T H E   M

B L A C K

M E N

- offering explanation and suggested solutions of how to avoid the many pitfalls facing young Black men in contemporary Britain.

A book by Lee Pinkerton

ii

RUNAWAY
SLAVE

"Emancipate yourself from mental slavery, none but ourselves can free our minds."

iv

"You must educate yourself in the problems of life. People with the least understanding have the most trouble."

Acknowledgments

This book is dedicated to my mother Norma Pinkerton,
my grandparents Donald and Irene Percy (R.I.P),
and the pioneers of the Windrush generation.

I'd also like to thank Ethelrene Percy for her proof reading and editing skills,

Derek Bardowell, Pascoe Sawyers, Nicola Rollock and Leyla Mehmet for their help and advice in trying to get this book published,

and Al Rasheed Dauda for his encouragement in embracing the social media, so vital in promoting my writing.

Author Biography

Lee Pinkerton was born in London at the end of the 1960s, the child of Jamaican and Guyanese immigrants. After leaving home at the end of the 80s to study Sociology and Psychology at University, he became seduced by the bright lights and glamour of the music industry and spent the next decade as a music journalist, first as a freelancer for magazines such as *Mix Mag*, *Echoes*, and *Hip-Hop Connection* and then as the Arts Editor for *The Voice* –'Britain's Best Black newspaper'.

It was whilst in this capacity that he interviewed such Hollywood stars as Samuel Jackson, Denzel Washington, Halle Berry, and Morgan Freeman. At this time he also appeared on music industry panel debates, and was a regular on-air contributor to radio stations Choice FM and BBC Radio London.

In addition to this he also wrote a book, *The Many Faces of Michael Jackson* published by Ozone books in 1997.

But as the 90s gave way to the Noughties, and Lee entered his 30s, the glamour of the film and music industries lost some of their sheen and he yearned to do something more substantial. Not only that, but now married with children he became concerned for the welfare of his two sons up growing up in London's poorest borough. So he left the cut and thrust of the media and the city of London taking his family to Derby in the East Midlands where they made their new home.

In 2006 he returned to University, again studying Psychology but this time at Master's degree level, and for a time was working in the area of mental health. But his passion for writing would not leave him and he has expanded the topic of his Master's degree research project into his latest book. Drawing on his own experiences and observations working in Prisons and in Psychiatric hospitals after leaving the media, as well as extensive academic research *The Problem With Black Men* examines the causes of the social problems facing Black men in Britain and America today.

His latest writing can also be found on the blog-site **theblakwatch.wordpress.com,** and his daily musings can be found on twitter **@_Runawayslave.**

CONTENTS

Preface xv

Introduction xxi

Putting it in context – Just what is the Black British Community?........................xxix

Problem 1 – Family Breakdown

The Black family - an endangered species?.2

Black Family Breakdown Throughout the Diaspora 7

Evolution of the Breakdown 11

Black man shortage 14

Absentee fathers
– the Babyfather syndrome 20

Teenage pregnancy and promiscuity 31

Solutions..35

References for Chapter 1.....................41

Problem 2 – Educational Underachievement and the exclusion crisis 43

The History of Race in Education.............48

The Triple Whammy of Disadvantage......49

School exclusions – the facts and cause....59

In School Factors 62

Out of School Factors 69

Solutions 73

References for Chapter 2 77

Problem 3 – Under-employment
- Surplus to requirements?......................81

Unemployment statistics ……...………...90
Historical Context …………….………..94
Gender Differences …………………...…96
Comparison with Asian immigrants……...99
What about self-employment?…………..102
The Black Work Ethic …………………......106
Level playing field? …………….……...112
Solutions …………………………………...122
References for Chapter 3 ……………126

Problem 4 – Crime
–Dying for respect?...............................129

Black on Black crime ……...………....134
The Crime Stats …………………..…...138
Street Gangs...……………………......…142
Dying For Respect ……………………148
The causes of crime and the government's
ineptitude …………………………………153
Solutions ……………………………….......162
References for Chapter 4 …………...…164

**Problem 5 - Mental Health
– Is Britain driving us mad?**...................**167**

The Stats ....…..............172
Examining Schizophrenia ....…...…176
Isolating The Causes ....…185
Solutions 194
References for Chapter 5….....…...........196

CONCLUSIONS ....…........**203**

Preface

The spur to write this book was a very personal one. I started it when I was 40 years old, unemployed, in debt and wondering where it had all gone wrong. From outside appearances I may have looked reasonably successful, but in my own eyes I was far from the levels of achievement that my early childhood promise had suggested. But I was not just wallowing in self-pity. Ironically, although I hadn't been in stable employment (meaning a contracted job as opposed to self-employment or freelancing) for over six years I was still the most successful man in my extended family. By the virtue of the fact that I had been to university, was married, owned my own house and my own car, I was by far the most accomplished. For my nine male cousins, (six resident in Britain three in America) unemployment and familial instability was the norm. Those dreams of high flying careers in law and medicine that had been the aspirations of our grandparents and had been embraced by our fellow Asian immigrants had been long since abandoned by us. It seemed that for a Black man in Britain, just avoiding an early death, a life of crime or residency on a psychiatric ward were the only achievements we could take pride in. The lack of any real success amongst the men in my family and the other Black men I saw around me let me know that my own lack of achievement was not down to my own shortcomings alone, but something more pervasive. My nine male cousins and I weren't some strange aberration, we were following a trend.

Mine was the traditional upbringing of British-born children of Caribbean immigrants. My grandfather came to Britain in the 1950's full of hope to make a better life for his wife and nine children. His seven daughters did relatively well all finding employment in the National Health Service, which was one of the biggest employers of Caribbean immigrants at the time. His two sons fared less well though. Not being academic enough to become doctors and not wanting to take the menial job of hospital porter, the NHS offered them no openings (male nurses were yet to be invented back in the 60's and 70's). So throughout the years that should have been their productive working lives they drifted between petty crime, self-employment and unemployment, the youngest son spending his latter years in self-imposed exile, so bitter and isolated from the rest of his family that he refused even to attend his own father's funeral. My grandfather must have wondered in his last days, as I do today, why his daughters had flourished whilst his sons had floundered. The sad fact was that as the Black men of his sons' generation came of age and entered the job market they had become surplus to requirements. Whilst the country was crying out for foreign labour in the 1950's to help rebuild the country and bolster the male workforce that had been decimated in the Second World War, by the 70's and 80's all the job vacancies had been filled. There was now a surplus of labour and the strong backs, and eager hands of the sons of Caribbean immigrants were no longer required. But somehow the Caribbean daughters still managed to make their way.

My contemplations were made all the more acute by the fact that I too had fathered two sons (but without the accompanying seven daughters). How was I to advise them how best to succeed in life when I clearly had not yet worked it out myself? Evidently education was not the simple answer that the first generation had thought, as my own relative academic success but lack of career advancement had proved. And either consciously or subconsciously the current generation seemed to have realised that too, as more and more seemed unwilling or unable to complete even basic schooling. And with each passing year the situation seems to grow worse.

Where my grandparents' and parents' generation had to be wary of attacks from racists teddy boys and the skinheads that followed them a generation later, my own sons have to be wary of youths who look just like them. This current generation of Black youth has become so alienated, so venal, and so distant from any way of achieving real success in the mainstream, that they have created their own warped value system in which they distinguish themselves in the street and gain respect through robbing, or murdering or gang raping other teenagers who look just like them. The children and grandchildren of African and Caribbean immigrants who would have regarded themselves as brothers and sisters in arms, colleagues at work, brethren and sistren in the church, united in the face of a hostile unwelcoming country, are now deadly enemies because they happen to live in a different post code or are members of a different gang.

The topic of my research project when I was studying my Masters degree in Psychology was investigating the over-representation of mental illness in general and schizophrenia in particular amongst the Black community in Britain. From my research I found that there was no single reason for the disproportion. Contrary to my expectations, it wasn't due to the alienation of living in a foreign land, or to the toll of daily racism that one faced as the child of an immigrant, or even to the racist preconceptions of the medical staff. There are a myriad of contributory factors why one would have a mental breakdown and they are all interconnected. My investigation into mental illness now makes up chapter five of this book. The other reasons that I feel are the contributory factors of our sorry state in this country make up the other four chapters.

This book is an attempt to find the root of the problem and offer a way out of the wilderness, so that our boys will fare better than their fathers and grandfathers did.

Introduction

At the start of 2008 a friend of mine predicted that it would be the year of the Black Man, and as the year evolved he was proved to be right.

It was the 40 year anniversary of **Martin Luther King's** assassination, but it was also the year the world had its first year Black F1 racing champion **(Lewis Hamilton),** the year a Black man captained the England football team (**Rio Ferdinand**), and the first Black man to manage a premiership football team (**Paul Ince**). Most significantly it was the year that **Barack Obama** became the first Black President of the United States. When Obama won the Presidential election, Black people the world over were filled with pride and new hope. On the morning after his election victory I like many others received this text message.

Rosa Parks sat,
so that Martin Luther King could walk,
so that Barack Obama could stand,
so that our children can fly.

But were Black people right to feel such pride? Barack Obama can be claimed by whites just as much as he is by Blacks. He is infact of dual racial heritage, as is Lewis Hamilton, and Rio Ferdinand. And Obama was not part of that American civil rights legacy of struggle. None of the ancestors on the Black side of his family came to America in slave ships, they were never cotton pickers or share croppers, and they never marched for freedom in the 60's. When his African father met his white mother it was as an overseas student at the University of Hawaii. Obama spent only a matter of days with his father and was raised by his white mother and his white grandparents. It occurred to me that maybe it was because of his unique racial heritage that he had the confidence to run for President when no-one gave him a chance. He didn't listen to all those people, (particularly Black ones, myself included) that said a Black man could never be President. Just like those who said that 'Black men don't play Golf' before **Tiger Woods** came along, or that 'F1 racing is not a Black man's sport' before Lewis Hamilton. Maybe it was because he wasn't hampered by those shackles of mental slavery that he was able to succeed so spectacularly.

As Bob Marley sang,

Emancipate yourself from mental slavery, none but ourselves can free our minds.

But what about the rest of us? Can the success of Obama, and Hamilton, and Ferdinand inspire Black men throughout the diaspora to new heights? We sure as hell hope so, because aside from those success stories, most ordinary Black men are struggling. We are **over-represented** in all the places that we don't want to be – the school exclusion figures, the young offenders institutions, the prisons, and the psychiatric units – and **under-represented** in all the places we should be - university graduation ceremonies, in the boardrooms, at the business breakfasts and business dinners, at the school parents' evenings, on the schools' boards of governors, even in the park playing ball with our sons.

In the States 47% of the penal population is African-American, but only 3.5% of the college students. We are 37% of the schools suspensions and have the lowest life expectancy. We have the highest homicide and cancer rates, and over 30% of the African-American males between 18-25 are unemployed.

This book's original working title was *The Problem with Black People*, but on further consideration I realised that the problems that face our race seem to be concentrated mainly with our men folk. It is predominately Black men not Black women who are the absentee parents, it is predominantly Black boys not Black girls who are in gangs and inflicting knife and gun violence on their neighbours. It is Black boys more than Black girls who are failing at school, and it these same Black boys who are getting dragged into the criminal justice system in numbers that far outweigh their proportion of the population.

In the introduction to his excellent book *Outliers,* another high achiever of mixed parentage **Malcolm Gladwell** argues that when looking at success stories we should not ask 'what are they like?' but rather examine the circumstances of their birth for clues to the secrets of their success. In my examination of the failure of Black men I will do the same thing and argue that when we look at the many areas in which Black men are failing, we should not look at the particular failings of these individuals, but instead look at the circumstances of their birth for clues to the origins of this malaise that blights the Black community. This is not to let off the hook those Black men who are bad fathers, or gang members, or drug dealers, or prison inmates, but rather to understand the phenomenon. Once we can understand the causes of the problem we can go about changing it.

I have separated what I see as the Black community's main problems into five areas and will address each problem in turn with its own chapter. At the end of each chapter I will offer solutions – things that can be done on a personal individual level to improve the situation. For each of these topics there are those that argue that the root cause is institutional racism. Black boys are excluded from schools in such numbers because of the racism of the teachers. They enter the penal system in such numbers because of the racism of law enforcement officers, and are misdiagnosed as schizophrenic because of the racism of mental health professionals. They struggle to find employment because employers are unwilling to employ Black men, and thus contribute to the break-up of the Black family because whilst Black men are denied access to the world of work, Black women are let through, and are thus leaving their Black men behind. All of these explanations maybe true, but if we just blindly accept them then we are accepting the role of mere victims. We are giving all the power to 'the other man', and there is nothing that we can do except to ask very politely if the white man would be so kind as to remove his foot from our necks! I for one am tired of waiting for a kindly white man to come along and save us. That is why, whilst acknowledging the role that white racism has to play, I am putting the onus firmly on Black folks, as the causes of and the solutions to our problems.

Throughout this book there is much reference to the American experience – I make no apology for that. Since our grandfathers arrived here in the 50's we as

Black Britons have long been looking elsewhere for our sense of identity, to other parts of the diaspora where our brothers in arms show more dynamism or confidence. Though we may have taken inspiration from the political, sporting and artistic success of our American cousins, the downside of our wholesale consumption of their culture is that many of the malaises that affect the African American population tend to visit themselves on us some years later. It is also to remind us that despite the high profile success of Black men like Chris Rock, Tiger Woods, Will Smith, Jay Z, and Barack Obama, the reality for the majority of African American men is very different.

Putting it in context – Just what is the Black British Community?

Though there has been an African presence in Britain since Roman times, the wave of mass immigration from the former colonies of the Empire began shortly after the Second World War.

Under the British Nationality Act 1948, large groups of post war economic immigrants came from the poorer Commonwealth territories, which included the Caribbean. Under this Act, citizens of the British Commonwealth were allowed to enter Britain freely in order to find work and settle. Many chose to take-up this option as a result of government led recruitment schemes by London Transport and the National Health Service, which is where many of these Caribbean immigrants found work. Immigrant populations have been historically drawn to the UK by labour shortages in particular areas – whether road-building in the early 20th century, health and transport services in the 1960s, or the textile industry in the 1970s.

Despite official encouragement, the entry into Britain of Black settlers began relatively slowly – a few hundred in 1948-1950, about 1,000 in 1951, about 2,000 in 1952 and again in 1953. 1953- 56 was seen as the years of highest level of influx.

Given their political history, firstly as part of the British Empire and then the Commonwealth, as well as the government led recruitment campaigns, the first immigrants naturally expected to be welcomed with open arms. But the response of the indigenous population was somewhat less warm, many immigrants being met with open hostility and discrimination. Though they were being actively recruited by such bodies as London Transport and the British Hotels and Restaurant Association, the Cabinet of the time still saw the entry of Black people as an ominous problem. The Commonwealth Immigrants Act of 1962 was the first in a long series of legislative measures attempting to restrict immigrants from the darker nations of the Commonwealth.

The history of the Caribbean population in this country over the last 60 years is one that has been characterised by resistance against racism and discrimination, and demands for equality and acceptance. Demands which were eventually enshrined in law by the Race Relations Act in 1976 and further addressed in the 80's by the Scarman Report into the Brixton Riots (Scarman 1981) and in the 90's by the inquiry into the murder of Black teenager Stephen Lawrence (Macpherson 1999).

In the census of 2011 the UK population was estimated at 60 million. The size of the minority ethnic population was estimated to be 12 million, or 14 per cent of the total population. The majority of this Black and minority Ethnic population (7.5%) is made of up of immigrants from the Asian sub-continent (Indian, Pakistani, Bangladeshi, and Chinese). The portion of that ethnic population made up of Africans and Caribbeans was estimated to be 3.3% per cent. It is surprising that Africans and Caribbeans are such a small proportion of the population considering the amount of attention we garner. For the purposes of this book when I talk of 'Black' people I am not including our fellow immigrants from the Asia. Though they have been our brothers-in-arms in the battle against discrimination, the terrible problems that now so blight our community, do not trouble them in the same way. Through the Black community's success in the fields of sport and entertainment we seem to have integrated more fully into British society, (indeed it was the assessment of the 2011 Census that the fast growing 'Mixed race' category was composed mainly of couplings between indigenous whites and Afro-Caribbean, rather than Asian immigrants). But the Asians' more inward looking community seem to have provided them more protection from the harsher effects of institutionalised racism. The Asian traditions of entrepreneurialism and self-employment insulated them from the ravages of mass unemployment visited upon African and Caribbean men during the last two recessions. It was Afro-Caribbean boys and men who were victims of the racist police practices in the 70's and 80's, and whilst Black men were stereotyped in the media as violent rapists and muggers, the Asians were looked upon as a group of passive and law-abiding, hard-working shopkeepers. And it is now Black boys not Asian boys who top the tables for school exclusion figures.

But it would be wrong to think of Britain's Black community as one homogenous lump. In the last few decades, it has undergone changes just as the wider British population has. Those pioneering African-Caribbean immigrants have given birth to children and grandchildren who have been joined by immigrants from the African continent. (The 2011 Census asserted that the fastest growing racial group born outside of Britain is from Nigeria). As well as some economic migrants following the lead of their Caribbean cousins, many came to study and then return home, or were asylum seekers fleeing from violence and persecution in their own country. And then there are those born of the mixed relationships between immigrants and the indigenous population. In fact at the end of the first decade of the 21st century, one of every two Black children born in Britain has a white parent. The make-up of modern Britain's Black community can be seen clearly in the English Football League. The many Black players to be found in the Premiership tend to be either imports from Africa (Yaya Toure, Michael Essien, John Mikel Obi), or products of bi-racial pairings in this country (Rio Ferdinand, Theo Walcott, Ashley Cole). Though coming from very different backgrounds, all are regarded as Black.

But despite the diversity of these varying backgrounds and personal histories, these African, Afro-Caribbean, Black British and bi-cultural children find themselves in pretty much the same boat – away from the football field, disproportionately concentrated in the lower echelons of society occupying particular positions of disadvantage in the UK. We generally have higher rates of unemployment, live in poorer housing, and are over represented in prison statistics. For example, recent evidence on school exclusions indicates that African Caribbean boys are three times more likely to be excluded than their white counterparts. Unemployment statistics show that African and Caribbean men and those from mixed backgrounds are between 15 and 20 per cent more likely to be unemployed than their white counterparts. This book will attempt to explain the causes for such disadvantage.

PROBLEM 1
The Breakdown of the Family

The Black Family
– an endangered species?

*"I never understood planned parenthood,
Cos I never met anyone who planned to be a
parent in the hood."*
Kanye West – The Joy

Introduction

Let me tell you the story of a female friend of mine, lets call her Lexine. An attractive Black woman when I first met her she was in her mid-twenties and had a young son of primary school age. She had a good job in the media, but was still struggling financially because she had no support from the child's father, who we'll call Barrington. This man was her first love, her first serious relationship when she was just 19. But sadly Lexine discovered that she wasn't <u>his</u> one and only love, for Barrington was what they call a 'playa'. Lexine wasn't prepared to be just one of his many 'babymothers', so shortly after their son was born, Barrington took no further part in either of their lives. Despite these challenges Lexine did the best she could to provide for her son, as well as ensuring that he had access to some positive male role models. But just as her son was preparing to enter secondary school, Lexine made the same mistake again and fell pregnant to another man of questionable commitment. He wasn't even based in this country full time when she started seeing him, and though there was talk of her going to live with him, or him coming over to live with her, when I visited her when the baby was a few weeks old, he still hadn't even seen his newborn. Though I tried to offer her some moral support I just couldn't understand why an otherwise intelligent and conscious Black woman would choose to make life so

2

hard for herself and her children. The first mistake we could put down to youthful naivety, but to do the same thing again in her thirties? If she was struggling financially before, it would now only get harder, as she had to take some time off work, and would incur large childminding fees if she chose to return. And as for her first born son, just as he was entering his challenging teenage years, falling less under the influence of his mother and succumbing more to the pressure from his peers, she would have less time and energy to give him as she turned her attention to her newborn. I lost touch with Lexine shortly after that, but I often wonder how her eldest son turned out. Did he stay the polite and well behaved boy that I first met, or did the lack of a father and the distracted attention of his mother lead him into the myriad of problems faced by so many of our young men?

I saw the same story unfold from the other perspective from one of my male friends. Abiola already had a child when she started going out with my friend Francis. She told him quite early on that she wanted to have another child, but Francis didn't pay that any mind – he was in his 20's and all about having some fun. He wasn't ready to settle down. But whether Francis was ready or not Abiola got her wish, and a few months into their relationship she fell pregnant.

Francis stayed by her all through the pregnancy and was there at the birth, but due to constant arguments he realised early on that this was not the woman he wanted to spend the rest of his life with, and their relationship ended soon after the birth. Francis has since married and had children with another woman, but he bent over backwards to maintain a civil relationship with Abiola, so that he could maintain a relationship with their son. Obviously it has been a strain having to provide finances as well as time and energy to two different children, from two different mothers, living in two different households, not to mention managing the emotional tensions between the two women, but Francis continues to endure it because he wants to be a more responsible father than his own dad was.

The story of Lexine and Abiola both with their two boys from two different fathers neatly encapsulates the problem with so many Black families. Yes many Black fathers are 'wutless' and irresponsible, but why would a woman choose to have a child with a man who's support she cannot rely on? You wouldn't buy a house with someone you didn't trust to pay their half of the mortgage or set up a business with someone who you couldn't rely on to pull their weight, so why would you have a child with one? Strangely it seems that Black women put their female friends under closer scrutiny, or put more effort into finding a suitable flat mate than they do in selecting a suitable father for their children.

Unfortunately too many Black women don't include men in their planning for a family. They are looked on as little more than sperm donors, selected on their good looks and 'good' hair, and little else. Even if the man does try and do the right thing and stay with the woman, his efforts are often frustrated by her own resistance and lack of respect. Their experiences with their own fathers have taught them that all Black men are no good and can't be relied upon, so they figure they can manage without them. And they do manage pretty well for the first few years, but when the boys start to turn into men themselves and problems other than the purely financial ones start, these single mothers don't know what to do. As mental health nurse **Eric A. Adjaidoo** explained when I interviewed him for background on Chapter 5 of this book.

"There was one time I had 33 clients who were African Caribbean men, and out of this 33 there was only 4 of them who were in regular contact with their father. It's a major problem that nobody likes to speak about it. A lot of Black mothers will argue 'we don't need a man', but its not the mothers who need a man, it's the children. By the time the boys are 12, 13 they are bigger than their mothers, they can stand up to

5

their mothers if they want to. That's when you need a father. There is a lot of stress in our young Black

men and I think that our young men are not strong enough mentally to deal with the stress. So many of our young people, as soon as they get a little bit of stress, they tip over."

Between 1972 and 2007 there was a dramatic rise in the number of households consisting of a mother living alone with one child – from 2% to 7%. This means that in 2007 there were 910,000 only children living with a single mother. If you throw in single dads that's over a million kids living with a single parent. These figures are for the UK population as a whole. As we know the situation in the Black community is much more acute. **Around a quarter of mothers of Caribbean origin are aged under 20 when their first child is born and the majority of these are single parents** (Robson and Berthoud 2003). For a long time it has seemed as though the family headed by a single female is the norm rather than the exception.

The Black family is in crisis. It is under threat from numerous interrelated factors. For various reasons there is a shortage of men, and when there are more females than males, this tends to lead to irresponsibility on behalf of the men. This leads to a preponderance of female headed households and the lack of male role models has two negative effects on the children. It leads to teenage boys running rampant, and teenage girls becoming sexually active at an earlier age, and them in turn starting their own female headed households where the vicious cycle can continue. Whilst these teenage boys with no father figures, run amok, seeking male companionship and protection in gangs, become involved in crime and get excluded from school, their chances for succeeding in mainstream society grow smaller and smaller. Those few Black girls who can resist the negative pull of their low budget environments and manage to succeed in education and then the job market will find themselves unable to find a Black male partner on a par.

Black Family Breakdown throughout the disapora
Unlike the gangs and gun crime, the breakdown of the Black family is not a new situation that has sprung up in Britain over the last couple of generations. Throughout the diaspora in America, Britain, or the Caribbean – wherever you find the descendants of slavery - the situation is the same.

U.S.A

The Early Years of Marriage (EYM) project followed 174 white couples and 199 Black couples in and around **Detroit Michigan**, after they married in 1986. In 2002, 16 years after the project began, 46 percent of the couples had already divorced, but the couples' race seemed to make a big difference. Just over a third (36%) of the white couples had divorced but **more than half (55%) of the Black couples had dissolved their marriages**. Why were the Black couples more prone to divorce? On average the black couples had cohabited for a longer period and were more likely to have had children before getting married. They also had lower incomes and were more likely to come from broken homes, and all of those influences are positively correlated with one's risk of divorce (Popenoe & Whitehead, 2004)

U.K.

The divorce of married parents is only one way a child may grow up in a single parent household, and not necessarily the most damaging. **The Social Justice Policy Group's report "Fractured Families"** looked at the role of family breakdown in pathways of disadvantage and drew attention to three distinct but overlapping forms of family breakdown.

1) Dissolution – where parents part after having children together.

8

2) Dysfunction – where parents are not able to provide their children with a sufficiently nurturing environment

3) 'Dadlessness' - many of these dads have never committed to their children's mother and are unable to provide the essential security which children need as their identities form.

Caribbean

In **Barbados**, at the time of its 1990 census, only 30% of mothers between the ages of 15 and 49 were married. Of the unmarried mothers, a few – roughly 3% were divorced, but the vast majority had never been married. Much the same story exists in every West Indian nation where the illegitimacy rate ranges from 35 to 72 percent. Judith Blake who has studied **Jamaican** family life in great detail has noted that one-third of all mothers had no male partner at all, married or unmarried. When Blake interviewed Jamaican women she found that they were often deserted by the men who had fathered their children, and having a child by one man, their chances of marrying another were greatly reduced. Some women tried to adjust to this possibility by giving their children away to relatives so that someone else would raise them. So extensive was this farming out of children that by 1986 fewer than half of all Jamaican first born children were being raised by their mothers. The mother, lacking a husband, had to work, and as a result, grandmothers, not mothers, and certainly not fathers, raised many Black Jamaican children

Back in Britain **Camila Batmanghelidjh,** of the charity *Kid's Company,* said men were usually seen as the "irresponsible" ones who got girls pregnant and "walked off". But black women were also to blame as they had a culture of rejecting men and being "cruel" towards them, she said. Ms Batmanghelidjh, who advises Prime Minister David Cameron, was speaking to the influential Home Affairs Committee in 2006. The Commons committee, which was investigating young black people and the criminal justice system, was told **57% of black Caribbean children grew up in lone parent households, compared with 25% of white children**.

Ms Batmanghelidjh told the MPs: "I actually think the mothers are hugely responsible because they have created a culture where they can get rid of the adolescent boy. "They can get rid of the male partner, they can survive on their own. "Often people think it's the males who are the culprits, the irresponsible people who come along and make these girls pregnant and walk off. And they underestimate the level of rejection and cruelty from the females towards the males. I actually think the males are really vulnerable and it starts in adolescence. "The minute the adolescent boy begins to look slightly like a male and behave like a male, often the mother wants that young male banished from the house. A hate relationship often develops. "I really think we underestimate the vulnerabilities of young black men."

Decima Francis, from the *Boyhood to Manhood Foundation*, echoed these concerns about the place of Black men in the family. "At the moment our men are like bees. Once they reproduce they are of no use - and they are dying,"

Evolution of the breakdown
So how did it come to this? Slavery weakened and destroyed families just as it impoverished and oppressed individuals. W.E.B. Du Bois made this claim in his 1908 book *The Negro American Family,* and E. Franklin Frazier enlarged on it in his 1939 book *The Negro Family in the United States.* For our enslaved ancestors there could exist no families in the nuclear sense of the word. A man, woman and child may live together, but they were not a family in any meaningful sense. The man may have fathered the child, but he had no exclusive sexual claim on the mother, he could not provide for her materially, and he had no right to prevent a slave sale from ending their union or from wrenching their child from them. As the historian Orlando Paterson argued, slavery prevented a

11

Black man from being either a father or a husband: he could offer to the mother and child "no security, no status, no name, no identity."

Historian Brenda Stevenson further elaborates on the effect of slavery on the Black family.

"Under slavery African-American women and not men were associated with children. When you look at a slave list and they list families for the most part they list the mother's name but not the father's. People didn't associate men with families – men were sold more often than women and they were sold at an earlier age."

What was left in such families as existed was the sense that the chief bond of a child was with its mother. What Patterson calls a "uterine society", one that some slave owners reinforced by a policy of separating more sons than daughters from their parents. As a result, slave women turned to their own mothers and their mothers' female relations rather than to their fathers for help.

More than 200 years after the end of slavery, money still continues to contribute to the break-up of the Black nuclear family. So much of the way that men identify and value themselves as fathers has to do with their ability to 'bread win'. Yet with Black male unemployment running at higher than the national average, many Black men are unable to find validation in this traditional role. For men without skills and qualifications, the situation is worse. There was a time when a man with a limited education but a strong back could count on finding plentiful physical work. Those days are gone. If a Black man finds that he cannot provide for his family he may feel, (and his partner may agree) 'what is the point of me being here?' And this may mean not just leaving the house but leaving the country. This has been the pattern in countless cases in this country, Black men trying to make a better life for themselves in America, or Canada, or Nigeria whilst their wives or ex-wives struggle to raise their children by themselves here.

There is a pattern in Black culture that might be called 'turning a negative into a positive', or 'making a virtue out of a necessity'. We take something that is awful and subvert it, rob it of its power to hurt or humiliate us, or even make it a badge of honour. This is the process by which pigs trotters, cows feet and other food that was thrown out by the slave master came to be celebrated as 'soul food', slave songs became gospel music, and as Leonard Pitts Jr. in his book *Becoming Dad* so artfully put it …

"the word 'nigger', the harshest epithet in the white racist lexicon, came to be embraced by some Blacks as a word denoting brotherhood.

"And thus did men castrated by their inability to do the things that would prove their manhood simply redefine

13

the equation, allowing themselves an attractive alternative to a standard which they could not reach."

So instead of being a husband and father they become a 'playa' if you're in America, or a 'Babyfather' if you're in Jamaica. Abandoned mothers became 'independent Black women 'who 'don't need no man'. And the nuclear Black family becomes the exception rather than the norm. So Black men, who through economic circumstances can take no pride in providing for their family, instead take pride in merely siring the children. Like a retired racehorse put out to stud, they boast of the number of children they have produced, (especially if they are boys) but seem to feel that their role begins and ends with conception. Once they have produced the child, they leave it to someone else to raise it (the mother, or the mother's family, or the state system), and this has been done for so many generations that many of us seem to have forgotten that this is not the way things should be done.

Man Shortage

Man shortage, all around the worl,
Girls are lonely and frustrated,
Man shortage, and so many lonely girls.
Crisis on the land', lonely lady caan't get a man,
Shortage, round the worlie worlie,
that's why every man haffe girlie girlie.
Man Shortage - Lovindeer

14

There is a serious imbalance between the number of Black men relative to the number of Black women on the mating market – an imbalance that gets more severe with time. There are many factors that contribute to this – rates of infant, childhood, adolescent, and adult mortality differ with men continuing to die at a faster rate throughout the lifespan. Far more men are imprisoned than women.

The estimated marital opportunities of Black women of different ages in the US in 1980 illustrate these cumulative effects. Adolescent women at the peak of their reproductive value have the greatest marital opportunities. At this age there are 108 men for every 100 women. By their late 20s the ratio has shifted. By ages 26-28 there are only 80 men for every 100 women. The ratio continues to decline as the women's reproductive value declines.

(David M. Buss - The Evolution of Desire)

The disparity between Black men and women
In the post slavery era, the economic parity of Black men and women continues. Due to the meagre wages of most Black males, women were forced to enter the labour market and contribute to the maintenance of the households. Such a strong economic role in the family had certain consequences for the marital relationship. The stability of the white, patriarchal family was based

15

on the economic dependence of the woman, forcing her into prescribed role of a passive, subordinate female. **Because Black females were more economically independent, many developed attitudes of freedom and equality unknown to most women in the 19th century**. Whilst this trait may be currently perceived as a healthy predecessor to the modern women's liberation movement, it produced tensions in Black marriages that were less prevalent in white marriages. **The independent woman, in the past and present, is more likely to be party to a dissolved marriage than her more reliant and passive counterpart.**
(Robert Staples – An Overview of Race and Marital Status)

It is not possible for every Black female college graduate to find a mate among her peers. Overall, the ratio of single college educated Black women to similar men is two to one. In certain categories the ratio is as low as 38 women to every male. It is among this middle class group that ideological preference – that is, the desire not to marry – is more prevalent. Because the women in this group earn 90 percent of a similar male's income, they do not need to marry for economic support. It is often the fulfilment of psychological needs that is the dominant reason for entering into marriage. But the greater a women's

16

educational level and income, the less desirable she is to many Black males. While a male's success adds to his desirability as a mate, it detracts from a womans'. Hence the women in this group are less likely to marry and remain married, if they do marry. It is a classical case of success in the labour market and failure in the marriage arena.

(Robert Staples – An Overview of Race and Marital Status)

In 1984 African-American husband and wife Sociologists Nathan and Julia Hare examined the crisis in their dramatically entitled book '*The Endangered Black Family – Coping with the Unisexualisation and Coming Extinction of the Black Race.*' Thankfully their predictions of the end of the Black race have not yet come to fruition, but much of their research is still pertinent.

This is how they summarised the situation in Black America in the mid 80's.

"The white woman has only to raise herself to the level of her man. If the Black woman moves up without a simultaneous escalation of the Black male, she will compound her isolation and too often look around to find that here is no strong Black man to stand beside her." (p 160)

"And many Black women, even now, if they had a good man who could support them and would; and if they thought the relationship would last, but it won't;

17

if only they could believe in the Black male, but increasingly they feel they can't: they'd trade the career, Mercedes and all, for the man."(p 139)

"The Black woman secretly knows that money is not enough. After she reaches a certain socioeconomic level, money loses some credit or value as a criterion of wellbeing...so that emotional support arises as the elusive craving of the thing that continues to elude her. (Hare & Hare 1984 p143)

Around that same time in the 1980's Gwen Gutherie sang *'Ain't Nothing Goin on But the Rent'*. The theme was updated in the 90's with TLC's *No Scrubs* and Destiny's Child's *Bills, Bills, Bills*. All these songs had a humorous tone but they also contained a kernel of truth –that no woman wants to have to financially support her man. And in truth most men do not feel comfortable being with a woman who earns considerably more than they do. So what's a Black women to do? She has three options.

1) the 'Rich white man' Option - go outside of her race in order to find a man on her economic level –

2) the 'Poorer Black man' Option - choose a man of her own race who may earn less that her and so deal with all the relationship tensions that will bring

3) the 'do without a man altogether' option

18

Economics has grave effects upon marital prospects for Blacks. The shift from an industrial to high tech economy has pushed a great number of Black males into unemployment. Job prospects have been decreasing for Black men in all age groups since 1955, while increasing for Black and white females. **This dismal fact leaves the Black woman** (with the exception of Black single mothers) **miles ahead of Black men in the labour force,** thus creating economic and social inequalities between the sexes.

The social rift between Black males and females begins at an early period of development. The same internal and external forces of family and society that encourage young Black females towards scholastic achievement discourage the young Black males from attaining the same goal. Society teaches Black males instead to prove their manhood through excelling in sports, music and hustling. Therefore some young black men learn early in life how to gain status in a system hostile to them.

Also during adolescence, there is often an increase in homicide, suicide, incarceration, and substance abuse among Black men. The depressing news about these threatening statistics is that **these circumstances leave a large number of Black women without Black partners.** What are the results? Black women focus more upon their education as a possible means of

19

economic, social, and sexual independence, instead of their reliance upon a man. Black men on the other hand seem confused today about how to provide the needs for the new Black woman who seems so self-sufficient.

It is suspected that as more Black women attend higher education and move further up in status, they may move away from Black men.......If Black males continue to be an endangered species through social oppression while some Black females continue

to succeed, there may be the potential for a tremendous gulf between the sexes

(Audrey B. Chapman. Male female relations – How the Past Affects the Present) .

Absentee fathers – the babyfather syndrome

"Papa was a rollin' stone,
wherever he laid his hat was his home,
And when he died,
all he left us was alone."
Papa Was A Rollin' Stone – The Temptations

Richard Dawkins is not a journalist, or a cultural critic, or a marriage counsellor. He is a Professor for the Public Understanding of Science at Oxford

University. In his famous book ***The Selfish Gene*** **(1976)** he spends less time discussing human relations than he does discussing animals genes and DNA, and when he discuss human interaction it is from a scientific evolutionary perspective, but it is very enlightening for the situation we find ourselves in today. In a nutshell he basically sees all human behaviour as a battle to ensure the survival of our genes. Richard Dawkins has probably never even heard of the term 'Babyfather' but in his book he gives a clear explanation in evolutionary terms of the behaviour of such men.

"If one parent can get away with investing less than his or her fair share of costly resources in each child, he will be better off since he will have more to spend on other children by other sexual partners, and propagate more of his genes.....

Ideally what an individual would 'like', would be to copulate with as many members of the opposite sex as possible, leaving the partner in each case to bring up the children."

Dawkins (1976) P140

Both partners ..want sons and daughters in equal numbers. To this extent they agree. What they disagree on is in who is going to bear the brunt of the cost of rearing each one of those children. Each individual wants as many surviving children as

21

possible. The less he or she is obliged to invest in any one of those children, the more he or she can have. The obvious way to achieve this desirable state of affairs is to induce your sexual partner to invest more than his or her fair share or resources in each child, leaving you free to have other children with other partners. This would be a desirable strategy for either sex, but it is more difficult for the female to achieve. Since she starts by investing more than the male, in the form of her large, food rich egg, a mother is already at the moment of conception 'committed' to each child more deeply than the father is…….

Therefore at least in the early stages of child development, if any abandoning is going to be done, it is likely to be the father who abandons the mother rather than the other way around.
Dawkins (1976) P 146

In 1948 78% of Black families in the US were headed by married couples. By the time the 90's had dawned that figure had fallen to 48% **A US census in the mid 90's found that 64 % of all African American children were growing up in one-parent households.** The Census Bureau reported that nearly half of all Black families are headed by a single mother. And this Babyfather syndrome is deeply ingrained in our culture.

In 2009 UK cable television station More 4 hosted a season celebrating the life and work of veteran civil rights campaigner and broadcast journalist **Darcus Howe**. One of the programmes entitled *Son of Mine* saw Howe trying to re-engage with one of his sons Amiri, after he had started to go off the rails in his late teens. At one point in the documentary, Howe like a typical Caribbean man, proudly declared that he had fathered seven children from three different women. Despite Howe's best interventions with his son, he seemed totally oblivious to the fact that him not being there for many of his son's formative years, may have played some contributory role in the troubles that the young man was now facing.

I witnessed a similar myopia from my own father when he re-established contact with me after an absence of over 20 years. Despite making very little effort to contact me throughout my childhood, and making absolutely no contribution to my upkeep – financial or otherwise – he flatly refused to admit he had done anything wrong or acknowledge that he had anything to apologise for. (That killed any chance of reconciliation between the two of us right there!)

But don't think that this attitude is confined only to old Caribbean men. Unfortunately the younger generation born in Britain have also inculcated it. In their paper ***Black Boys and schooling: an intervention framework for understanding the dilemmas of***

23

masculinity, identity and underachievement' authors
Tony Sewell and Richard Majors relate interactions
they observed between teachers and pupils from an
inner city boy's comprehensive school. The new Black
head-teacher related one particularly revealing
exchange he had with some Black boys in their
Personal Social and Education class.

"During a Social Education class, we were talking
about children's reading books and we were trying to
identify stereotypes. I told them I had 10 year old
twins, one boy, one girl, and my wife and I decided we
would not create the gender divide in the twins. Then
one of the boys in the class said to me: 'You've only
got two kids sir?

I said yes that's right.' He then asked: 'What about the
others back in Jamaica?'

I said 'I've only got two children'.

He said: Well sir, you're not really a true Yard Man!"

And just as young Black boys see it as the norm for
Black men to have children by multiple partners,
whilst caring for none of them, young Black women
see Black men as an unreliable source of support.

As one Black female respondent put it in *The
Endangered Black Family*.

*"I think we are aggressive and dominating and
domineering. But I think its because we've had to be.
Like out mothers before us and our grandmothers and*

24

great-grandmothers had to. You pick up from them. Cause mothers tell their daughters; ' you know he's not going to be able to support you, and you're going to go and have to get an education and help him. Cause you know how these men are'."
(Hare & Hare – 1984 p86)

Do fathers matter? / The Effect of no father

Well what does it matter? Hasn't the Black family since slavery traditionally been headed by a woman? Many Black women today seem to think that they can raise their sons perfectly well without the baby's father. Well I'm here to tell them, that they can't. A mother can love and care for her son, but she can't teach him how to be a man any more than she can teach him the correct way to shave. A perspective echoed by clinical psychologist Thomas J. Harbin in his 2000 book '*Beyond Anger – A Guide for Men.*

"...women do not know first-hand about being a man. They can only provide a female perspective on what being a man is all about. What's more, their knowledge about what it means to be a man has often come from the same confused men that we have been talking about: their fathers, husbands, brothers, and boyfriends. Women know what <u>they</u> want in a man. But this is not even close to a man teaching a boy what it means to be a man. A woman should not be the only source of instruction that a boy receives on how to be

a man. Asking a boy to learn about being a man solely from a woman is like asking an electrician to teach someone about plumbing."

(Harbin, 2000)

Yes Black women have been raising their children and heading their families single handedly for generations, but that is not a situation we should welcome. There are many examples in life of people who have achieved great things in their lives without the use of their legs, or their eyes etc. But it's not a situation they would choose for themselves had they been given a choice!

In 1996 a University of California study found that boys raised without their fathers are more than twice as likely to engage in delinquent behaviour and that girls in the same situation are more than twice as likely to become teenaged mothers. A 1998 study by researchers at Princeton University and the University of Pennsylvania said that young men are twice as likely to be jailed if raised without a father. According to **Levitt & Dubner** in their 2005 book *Freakonomics*, childhood poverty and a single parent household are the two biggest predictors that a child will have a criminal future. Growing up in a single parent home roughly doubles a child's propensity to commit crime, as does having a teenage mother. That's how significant the contribution of a father is.

What matters is not simply the presence or absence of a father in the childs' home, but their availability, involvement and the quality of the father child relationship. The National Family and Parenting Institute argue that this relationship is important for "childrens' greater self confidence, mental health, positive behaviour and relationships, educational attainment and cognitive skills."

In a study of 144 middle class white families in Virginia, USA **(Heerington, Cox and Cox, 1982)** half the children were from divorced, mother - custody families, and half from non-divorced families; their average age at separation was 4 years. After 1 year, most children from divorced families (and many parents) experienced emotional distress and behaviour problems associated with the disruptions in family functioning. This was much improved after 2 years; the main exception being that some boys had poor relations with their custodial mothers and showed more anti-social and non-compliant behaviour than boys from non-divorced families.

A follow up was made after 6 years, when the children had an average age of 10 years of separation. Mother daughter relationships were generally not much different from those in non-divorced families, however mother –son relationships continued to be rather tense for divorced mothers who had not remarried; even despite warmth in the relationship, sons were often non-compliant and mothers ineffective in their attempts at control.

In terms of early indicators of criminal behaviour, children who experience family breakdown in all its forms are twice as likely to have behavioural problems, perform less well in school, suffer depression and turn to drugs, smoking and heavy drinking. **(Rodgers, B & Prior, J. 1998, Divorce and Separation: The Outcomes for Children, JRF)**

UK journalist and educationalist **Tony Sewell** believes the problems that disadvantage Black boys in the schools and criminal justice system (which will be dealt with in more detail later in this book) all stem from the boys lack of a father. Sewell is the director of the charity **Generating Genius,** which attempts to raise the academic achievement of Black boys. One of the ways he attempts this is by running a residential summer camp, and Sewell detailed his struggles in one of his regular columns in the Guardian newspaper.

"...our academic ideals soon became secondary; many of the boys, once freed from the arms of their single mothers, suddenly had to cope with a world run by adult black males - figures in their lives who were mostly absent, unreliable, despised by their mothers, and usually unsuccessful.

We have wasted years, and lives, looking in the wrong direction as to the causes of crime and educational failure. We've had endless studies attempting to prove institutional racism – while all along our boys' psychological needs weren't met."

But it is not only the sons of absentee fathers who suffer – the daughters are affected too.

"On average a girl whose father divorces or separates from her mother and leaves the home before she is aged ten, comes into puberty six months earlier than a girl from an intact family; her body is physically changed by his absence. This pubertal precocity is not very helpful, because girls who arrive at puberty young are at greater risk of a host of later problems, including sexual promiscuity and teenage pregnancy. Fatherless girls are also liable to have negative attitudes to men and to declare themselves less interested in long term stable relationships. Nor is the impact of fathers limited to whether they are physically present. In intact families, girls reach puberty later if they have a positive rather than a negative relationship with their father, and the more he in involved in her care the later it is."

(Audrey B. Chapman. Male female relations – How the Past Affects the Present).

29

The psychologist Jay Belsky and his colleagues argue that harsh, rejecting and inconsistent child rearing practices, erratically provided resources, and marital discord foster in children a mating strategy of early reproduction and rapid turnover. In contrast sensitive, supportive and responsive child rearing combined with reliable resources and spousal harmony foster in children a mating strategy of commitment marked by delayed reproduction and stable marital bonds. **Children growing up in uncertain and unpredictable environment learn that they cannot rely on a single mate. They therefore opt for a sexual life that starts early and that inclines them to seek immediate resources from multiple temporary mates.** In contrast, children who grow up in stable homes with predictably investing parents opt for a strategy of permanent mating because they expect to attract a stable high investing mate. The evidence from children of divorced homes supports this theory. Such children reach puberty earlier, engage in intercourse earlier, and have more numerous sex partners than their peers from intact homes.
(Belsky, Steinberg, & Draper (1991). p217)

When one studies the biographies of recent sporting success like Lewis Hamilton in Formula 1, the Williams Sisters in Tennis, or Tiger Woods in Golf, we see these athletes repeatedly paying tribute to the efforts of their fathers, without who's input and dedication they wouldn't have reached such heights. We can only wonder how many more success stories we would have in the Black community, had more Black men made the effort to be involved fathers.

Teenage pregnancy and promiscuity

Mary had a little lamb, that's a fib,
She had two twins though, and one crib,
Now she's only 14, what a start,
But this effect is quite common, in these parts.
Ghetto Thing by De La Soul

Societies in which men are more numerous than women tend to have very different standards than those in which women outnumber men. A culture's sex ratio is a simple count of the number of men for every 100 women in a specific population. When the sex ratio is high, there are more men than women, and when the sex ratio is low there are fewer men than women. Cultures with high sex rations (in which there aren't enough women) tend to support traditional, old-fashioned roles for men and women (Pedersen, 1991; Secord, 1983). The women stay home raising children while the men work outside the home. Such cultures also tend to be sexually conservative. The ideal newlywed is a virgin bride, unwed pregnancy is

31

shameful, open cohabitation is rare and divorce is discouraged. In contrast, **cultures with low sex ratios (in which there are too few men) tend to be less traditional and more permissive. Women are encouraged to work and support themselves, and they are allowed (if not encouraged) to have sexual relationships outside of marriage. If a pregnancy occurs, unmarried motherhood is an option** (Barber, 2001).

Sounds very much like the Black community doesn't it?

The specifics vary with each historical period, but this general pattern has occurred throughout history. When sex ratios are high, there aren't enough women to go around. If a man is lucky enough to attract a woman, he'll want to keep her. And encouraging women to be housewives who are financially dependent on their husbands and discouraging divorce are ways to do just that. On the other hand, when sex ratios are low, there are plenty of women to go around, and men may be less interested in being tied down to just one of them. Thus, women work and delay marriage, and couples divorce more readily if dissatisfaction sets in.

From Intimate Relationships – Miller, Perlman and Brehm (fourth edition 2007)

In the Black community for reasons already outlined, there are always more women than men.

Much can be learned from studies where researchers talk at length to young women about their experiences. According to Sociologist Graham and Mc Dermott young women prioritize their relationships with their babies, over their often difficult relationships with the babies fathers because they feel this relationship is a more certain source of intimacy than the sexual relationship they had experienced.

The Marriage Gap thesis has emerged from the observation that after 1970 women at all income levels began to marry at older ages, but where mothers higher up the income scale put off having children until they were married, working or gaining degrees in the intervening period, women in the lowest strata did neither. As Hymowitz states, "the results radically split the experiences of children. Children in the top quartile now have mothers who not only are more likely to be married but are older, more mature, better educated and nearly three times more likely to be employed as mother in the bottom quartile". Moreover the children in the top quartile also get the benefit of more time and money from their live-in fathers. Children born at the bottom of the income scale have access to far fewer resources, including social capital, because their mothers are less established in their identities, they are less educated, poorer, and most

importantly are struggling to fill the shoes of absent fathers.
(Hymowitz, K., 2006).

If being born a Black boy in this country puts you at a disadvantage, then being a Black boy born to a teenage single mother puts you in a double disadvantage. In their 2005 book ***Freakonomics*** American authors Levitt & Dubner apply economic theory to everyday popular phenomena. . According to them childhood poverty and a single parent household are the two biggest predictors that a child will have a criminal future. In their chapter entitled 'What Makes a Perfect Parent? they isolated eight factors that are strongly correlated with a child's improved academic performance at school.

Among these 8 factors are obvious ones like:

The child has highly educated parents,

The child's parents have high economic status,

The child's parents speak English in the home,

The Childs parents are involved in the PTA,

And the Child has many books in his home.

but one of the more surprising factors was that

the child's mother was thirty or older at the time of her first child's birth.

"A woman who doesn't have her first child until she is at least 30 is likely to see that child do well in school.

This mother tends to be a woman who wanted to get some advanced education or develop traction in her career. She is also likely to want a child more than a teenage mother wants a child. This doesn't mean that an older first time mother is necessarily a better mother, but she has put herself – and her children – in a more advantageous position." **(Dubner & Levitt 2005)**

Conclusions & Solutions to Problem 1

So what have we learnt in this chapter?
57% of black Caribbean children grow up in lone parent households, compared with 25% of white children. It is clear that as part of the damaging legacy of slavery it has become part of modern day Black culture for women to take the lead role in raising children, and for men to take a back seat (if they remain seated at all). Women do not rely on the father of their children to help raise them, and too many men feel that their job is completed at the point when the sperm successfully fertilises the egg.

We have also learnt that **around a quarter of mothers of Caribbean origin in Britain are aged under 20 when their first child is born, and the majority of these are single parents**, but we have also discovered that a child's life chances are greatly enhanced if the mother is 30 or older before their first child is born. So a Black child born to a teenage single mother has the odds against it before it has even taken its first step.

Understand, that I am not running down single mothers – I myself was raised by one - but after the demise of her young marriage she returned to the home of her parents, and I was raised by not only my mother, but my grandparents, my aunts, my uncle and my elder cousins – traditional African village style. Things may have turned out very differently if she had chosen to stay in London, and attempt to raise me by herself without any support from her extended family.

We have seen the vicious circle forming before our eyes having learnt that **boys raised without their fathers are more than twice as likely to engage in delinquent behaviour and girls in the same situation are more than twice as likely to become teenaged mothers. Young men are twice as likely to be jailed if raised without a father.** We can see a clear link between the large proportion of Black families headed by a single mother and the large proportion of teenage criminals and single mothers. So unless we are happy to see so many of our young people waste their talents and throw away their lives we must put an end to the single parent families.

36

Easy to say but how???

1. Think very carefully about the suitability of your partner before having a child with them. Since once a woman falls pregnant it is ultimately her decision as to whether to keep the child or not, then men should interpret Solution number 1 as 'think very carefully about the suitability of your partner before having unprotected sex with them'. Many a man has gotten caught out like Francis in the introduction. They just wanted sex but the woman wanted a baby. Advice to all the brothers out there – there are only two foolproof ways of not impregnating a woman when she has set her heart on having a child. 1) Have a vasectomy. 2) Don't have sex with her. Contrary to what many women claim you DO need a man to help raise your child, regardless of how much financial support you are getting from the government. Being a suitable parent has nothing to do with being good looking, or being sexy, or stylish, or being funny, or driving a nice car. These may be reasons why you'd want to have sex with them, but these are not good criteria to have a child with someone. If it takes two of you to raise a child properly then that means that you will be binded together for at least 18 years. Ask yourself before you have unprotected sex, or when you are deciding whether to keep that unborn child, 'is the other person someone you want to tied to for the next two decades?'

'Is this someone I want to be teaching values to my child?' All too often the cause of marriage break ups is the fact that the two partners didn't really know each other in the first place. They may have known each other on a superficial level, but not on significant matters like politics, or religion/spirituality, attitude to managing money, how to raise their kids etc. Those problems they may be aware of, they overlook as insignificant because they are so much in love. Love is blind as the saying goes but once that glow of the passionate honeymoon period has dissipated, these are the things that can cause conflict, and the fact that he is tall and handsome, or she has a fit body, or he is a good dancer and dresses well, won't seem so significant!

2. Women – before falling pregnant think very carefully about if you are ready to have a child. As any parent will tell you, when you become a parent your interests come second and your child's come first. Or at least they should do! Everything from when and if you sleep, where you choose to live, when where and if you can afford to go on holiday, your social life, your choice of friends, - all of these things should take into consideration the best interests of the child. Are you mature enough to put your interests on the backburner? If not then you are not ready to bring a young life into the world. This is the 21st century with contraception freely available. Should people not ready, willing and able to provide a stable home for their children really be bringing new lives into the world by accident?

Regarding these first two points please understand exactly what I am advocating here. I am not promoting the institution of marriage, (although that is shown to be the best environment in which to raise a child). I am not advocating abstination from sex out of wedlock, or even abortion. What I am saying is DON'T HAVE A CHILD UNTIL YOU ARE IN A COMMITTED, LONG TERM RELATIONSHIP, AND THE TWO OF YOU ARE WILLING TO DEDICATE THE NEXT TWO DECADES OF YOUR LIVES TO RAISING THAT CHILD.

3. In an ideal world when you have a child with someone, you will be married to each other and have made a commitment to stay with each other 'till death do us part'. Unfortunately as we all know it doesn't always go like that. If you do bring a child into the world, and the relationship with the other parent breaks down, **don't let the fathers' relationship with the child break down also**. Women don't use the child as a weapon to hurt the ex who hurt you. And men, don't abdicate your responsibility to your child because you are no longer getting along with the mother. The two of you need to put your emotions aside and be mature and responsible for the child's sake. And women, if he really is such a bastard, men if she really is such a bitch, what were doing having sex with them in the first place? What does that say about you?

4. The best way to prevent your teenage daughter getting pregnant is not to give them a serious talk, or ban them from having boyfriends, **but instil into them some ambition.** No girl is going to allow herself to get pregnant at 16 if she knows it will prevent her from going to university and realising her dream.

References for Chapter 1 - Family Breakdown

Belsky, Steinberg, & Draper (1991). Childhood experience interpersonal development and reproductive stategy. An evolutionary theory of socialisation. *Child Development 62*, 647-670

Biddulph. S (2003) *Raising Boys*. Harper Thorsons

Buss, D. M. (1994) - *The Evolution of Desire* Basic Books

Chapman, A. B. Male female relations – How the Past Affects the Present .
in *Black Families* (second edition)1988 edited by Harriette Pipes McAdoo. Sage Publications. London.

Dawkins, R. (1976) *The Selfish Gene.* Oxford University Press. Oxford

Dubner, S.J and Levitt, S.D.. (2005). *Freakonomics – A Rogue Economist Explores the Hidden Side of Everything..* Penguin. London

Harbin, T. J. (2000) '*Beyond Anger – A Guide for Men'.* New York. Malowe & Company

Hare, N. & Hare J. (1984). *The Endangered Black Family – Coping with the Unisexualisation and Coming Extinction of the Black Race.* Black Think Tank. (San Francisco)

41

Hymowitz, K., (2006) *Marriage and Caste in America: Separate and Unequal Families in a post-marital age.* Ivan R Dee

James, O. (2006) *They Fuck You Up*: *How To Survive Family Life*. Bloomsbury Publishing PLC

Kunjufu J. (1999) *Countering the Conspiracy to Destroy Black Boys Vol III.* African American Image. Chicago, Illinois.

Pitts, L. (1999) *Becoming Dad – Black Men and the Journey to Fatherhood*. Agate Books. Canada

Rodgers, B & Prior, J. (1998) *Divorce and Separation: The Outcomes for Children,* JRF

Staples R – *An Overview of Race and Marital Status in Black Families* (second edition)1988 edited by Harriette Pipes McAdoo. Sage Publications. London.

Miller, Perlman and Brehm *Intimate Relationships* (fourth edition 2000) p13-14

Wilson, J.Q. (2002) Slavery and the Black Family in *The Marriage Problem.* Harper Collins

PROBLEM 2
Educational Underachievement and the exclusion crisis.

"Build your penitentiaries, we build your schools.
Brainwash education, to make us the fools."
Slave Driver - Bob Marley

"Lessons I was taught are quick to fade,
Soon as I realised that turning papers in won't get me paid."
Underground Kings – Drake

"The 13,000 people excluded from school each year might as well be given a date by which to join the prison service sometime later down the line."

Martin Narey, Chief executive of Barnados and former Director General of HM Prison Service. 2001

"Racial inequalities in the education system do not just mirror the inequalities in society, they entrench them, passing them onto another generation."

DfES (2006). *Exclusion of Black Pupils: Priority Review: "Getting It. Getting it Right."*

As I stated in the introduction to this book, the explanations for most of the social problems that blight the Black British population fall roughly into two camps. One camp suggests that the root cause of our problems is institutional racism, where the other camp argues that in fact Black people themselves are to blame, our problems caused and perpetuated through some defect present within us. Nowhere is the dichotomy clearer or more angrily debated than in the topic of the educational underachievement of Black boys. There are even some academics and activist who refuse to use the term 'underachievement' as this suggests that the problem is with the pupils themselves as opposed to there being wider problems with the education system.

Then there are others, the most high profile of them being Dr Tony Sewell, who feel that focussing our attention on racism from individual teachers or even at an institutional level is detracting attention from the true source of the problem - the boys themselves, and the anti-education subculture that has grown up amongst Black youths. In this chapter I will examine both perspectives.

I myself endured more than my fair share of racism whilst at school. Due to the efforts of my mother, I went to a primary school in a nice middle class area that also happened to be exclusively white. No Asians, no Blacks, no mixed raced pupils, - just a school full of white kids and me. I wasn't exactly welcomed with open arms. During my first year there I endured racial abuse in the playground on a daily basis. This being the late 70s, my tormentors were supplied with a constant supply of verbal ammunition from the racial epiphets that were a weekly feature of our television schedules at the time, from comedians like Jim Davidson, and Bernard Manning, and racist sit-coms like *Love Thy Neighbour* and *Mind your Language*. I'm sure that the teachers were aware of the abuse that I suffered, but turned a blind eye. (Remember this was

45

the 70s when it was still socially acceptable (and legal) to be racist.)

I was hopeful when moving to secondary school as that was more racially mixed, however since the majority of the Black pupils went to the poorer inner city primary schools, they were automatically streamed into the 'B Band', whilst I and my white middle-class classmates from the better primary school were transferred smoothly into the 'A band'. So once again I found myself the only Black boy in the class. But since there was such a large Black presence in the school as a whole, racial abuse in the playground wasn't tolerated. (This now being the 80s the teachers still didn't intervene, but the white boys would have gotten a 'beat down'). Here the racism was a bit more subtle.

I will always remember one incident I had with a teacher. I was put in after-school detention by my French teacher, and whilst he and I sat in silence in the classroom, there was a commotion outside in the corridor. He went outside to tell the kids to stop messing about and clear off home, but as he came back into the classroom, I thought I heard him mutter something under his breath about 'bloody nig-nogs'. As I sat alone with him in the classroom silently in shock, my form teacher entered the room to ask what all the commotion had been about. There was no mistaking the response my French teacher gave.

'I don't know, some coon or other', he said, with neither of the teachers giving even a glance in my direction. If this was how they talked in front of me, how did they talk about their Black pupils in the privacy of the staff room I wondered? Needless to say I lost interest in French after that.

Despite these and other experiences at school, I passed through relatively unscarred. Despite the frequent playground fights that I had felt were essential to establish myself at primary school, I rarely got into trouble. Maybe because of my intelligence, or maybe because of my sporting talents, I was never suspended, never excluded, went onto the sixth form, and then onto university. Unfortunately the majority of Black Boys in Britain do not do so well.

In 2006 only 47.5% of Black pupils achieved 5 or more A to C grades at GCSE compared with 57.2% of white pupils (DfES 2006). The next year it went down to 44.9%. Similar patterns of inequality are evident in school exclusions figures with twice as many Black pupils permanently excluded from school compared with the national average.

History of Race in Education

The experience of Black children in British schools has been a concern since the sixties. In his 1971 book *How the West Indian Child Is Made Educationally Subnormal in the British School System*: Coard outlined how the first generation of Black school children faced open racism from staff and other pupils, discrimination in teacher assessment and culturally biased testing. They were frequently excluded from the mainstream after being deemed 'Educationally Subnormal', and many argue that the current disparity in exclusion rates for Black pupils is a modern manifestation of the same process that saw so many Black pupils classified as 'educationally subnormal' in the past.

The 1981 Education Act was introduced to provide an objective and consistent framework for the identification and support of those children with greatest need. However, it soon became clear that there was a trend towards legislation and special needs procedures being used in such a way as to hasten the removal of Black students from mainstream education. The recommendations of the Rampton (1981) and Swann (1985) reports were highly criticised but marked something of a watershed in public policy on race and education in Britain, by first rejecting IQ-ist notions of innate intellectual differences between the races, and second by stating that teachers (in their expectations and actions towards pupils and parents) might actively be implicated in the creation of race inequality.

Similarly in 1984 a survey within the Inner London Education Authority (ILEA 1984 Report 4627) showed that the over representation of Black students in special schools and units, tended to be within those categories that depended on the interpretative assessment of teachers and educational psychologists. Consequently, Black children were over-represented in schools for disruptive behaviour and language impairment.

Today Black boys are suffering a triple whammy of disadvantage – they are disadvantaged by their gender, often by economics and finally by their race.

The triple whammy of disadvantage
1) The Gender disadvantage
The problem of educational underachievement is again one that most acutely affects Black males. White boys are also doing worse than their female peers, but because the situation in our wider community is so critical, this educational underachievement is more urgent. Every year when examination results come out, the papers are full of the news that boys are falling

behind girls in terms of achievement. According to the **Higher Education Policy Institute report** published in **2009** there is an achievement gap between the sexes that starts at school but carries on into adulthood. The result is that men are less likely to go to university and less likely to do well when they get there. The study finds that 37.8% of men participate in higher education, compared to 49.2% for women. The trend exists for part time and full time further education across all ages and races and among the rich and poor. And at university, women continue to outperform men. There are various explanations offered by commentators. The **Higher Education Policy Institute's** report suggests that GCSE's appear to favour girls because of the style of teaching, content and types of question, and highlights the fact that boys' school performance began to lag behind at about the time the exams were introduced in the 1980s. However the exams can not be solely to blame, as the gender gap also exists in different countries with different systems. Another explanation often offered includes the lack of male teachers in the classroom, or the lack of male role models in the family as the reason for this underachievement. For Black boys we can add in the lack of role models in the community who have used education to as a means to their success, rather than a God given talent or street smarts.

In his book *Help Your Boys Succeed- the essential guide for parents* **Gary Wilson** addresses the problem. Wilson observes that the proportion of male teachers under the age of 30 in school, in the UK, both primary and secondary in the mid naughties was around 5 per cent. In fact almost half the pupils in primary schools in the UK will not be taught by a male teacher until they reach secondary school. As **Jawanza Kunjufu** in his book *Countering the Conspiracy to Destroy Black Boys Vol III* put it: *"when 83% of your teaching staff is white, and only 1.2 percent of your teaching staff is African American male, it is a very good chance that the group that's least represented (African American males) are going to receive the brunt of improper or inappropriate labelling."*

A reason commonly mentioned for the poor academic performance and alienation of some Black males is that they perceive most schooling activities as feminine and irrelevant to their masculine sense of self and development. (Holland 1989).

The predominantly white, middle class, female teachers impose feminine standards of behaviour on the class room, that the working class Black Boys are least likely to meet and that will lead to conflict and oppositional behaviours in academic attitude and engagement. Boy culture (not to mention Black culture) is marginalized and suppressed at best – devalued and destroyed at worst.

So if they are being taught by women in the classroom, and there is no man in the house who is involved with academia, and their own heroes and role models are succeeding in life by use of their sporting or musical talents, then how do they develop a love of learning, or grow to understand that education is something that they can use to help them attain their goals in life?

According to Wilson teachers will tell you that by and large, girls tend to be far more independent than boys when starting school. Boys arrive not being able to tie their own shoe laces or even button up their own coats. And this 'learned helplessness' carries over into their attitude to learning. It is said that 'women raise their daughters and mother their sons'. But if we do everything for our boys, argues Wilson, then we disadvantage them in so many ways, not least in their ability to become independent and successful learners

2) Economic disadvantage
Toby Young is a journalist and author, his most famous work being *How To Lose Friends and Alienate People*, which was made into a film starring Simon Pegg in 2008. Young was in the news in 2009 because he was hoping to take advantage of the Conservative Party's new education policy and create a 'free school'

in his local area. Whilst reading more about Young's own background I discovered that his father Michael Young (also known as Lord Young of Dartingdon) was a visionary educationalist who was a passionate advocate for comprehensive education in the 1960s and came up with the idea for the Open University. Toby himself had gained a first class honours degree from Brasenose College, Oxford and studied at Harvard and Trinity College, Cambridge. No big surprises there, most of the middle class elite that dominate politics and the media were educated at Oxford/Cambridge/Harvard/Yale including our own Prime Minister David Cameron and American President Barack Obama. But what is interesting and different about Young, is where he was educated before university. In the pictures that accompanied the 2009 newspaper article, he is pictured with his multi-racial classmates at Highgate primary school in 1974. Sitting alongside him in the front row are four Black boys. Toby reveals that he attended two mediocre comprehensives and failed all of his 'O' Levels. He then switched to the William Ellis grammar school and managed to get three 'A' levels and win a place at Oxford. I wondered if those Black pupils he left behind at Highgate Primary were fortunate enough to enjoy a similar intervention and go onto enjoy such career success. Somehow I doubt it. Whilst Toby Young went onto an international career as a journalist, author, and movie script writer the best that those Black boys could have hoped for, if they didn't display some musical or sporting talent, was a life of mediocrity and anonymity. That's if they could avoid the triple threat of jail, mental illness or a violent early death. But what separated Young from his Black classmates was not so much his race, but rather having a father with the resources to scoop his son out of the dead-end comprehensive and into a more productive grammar school, that could bring out from him the necessary grades to get into the university of the elite, when he realised that his grand educational experiment was going horribly wrong.

Black boys are doubly disadvantaged in school, firstly because they are male, and secondly because they will more than likely come from a lower income family. And this disadvantage begins even before they start school.

In the late 1990s, the U.S Department of Education undertook a massive research project called the **Early Childhood Longitudinal Study**. The ECLS sought to measure the academic progress of more than 20,000 children from kindergarten through to the fifth grade. The subjects were chosen from across the country to represent an accurate cross section of American school children. The data revealed that Black children who performed poorly in school did so, not because they were Black, but because they were more likely to come from a low-income, low education household. A typical Black child and a white child from the same socio-economic background however, were found to have the same abilities in math and reading upon entering kindergarten.

Back in Britain, according to research first published by the then education secretary Estelle Morris, a bright baby from a poor background is liable to be overtaken by a less bright baby from a wealthy background by the age of 22 months, boosted by educated parents and a stimulating home environment. In 2008 almost 30% of children on free school meals did not get five good GCSEs; two thirds of children from lower socio economic groups do not make it to A levels. Children on free school meals represent just 0.5% of all pupils gaining three A s at A level – essential for those wanting places at Britain's top universities. A 2010 report by the Office for Fair Access revealed that intelligent children from the richest 20% of homes in England were seven times more likely to attend a high-ranking university than intelligent children from the poorest 40%. A 2012 report from Ofsted observed that the previous year only a third of children from the poorest homes gained five good GCSEs compared with 62 % of other children.

Although good schools make a difference, the biggest influence on educational attainment, how well a child performs in school and later in higher education, is family background. In a report on the future of education in Britain, **Melissa Benn** and **Fiona Millar** describe how :-

"One of the biggest problems facing British schools is the gap between rich and poor, and the enormous disparity in childrens' home backgrounds and the social and cultural capital they bring to the educational table."

A 2005 Joseph Rowntree Foundation report concluded : *"The strength of the relationship between educational attainment and family income, especially for access to higher education, is at the heart of Britain's low mobility culture and what sets us apart from other European countries."*

3) Racial disadvantage

Even if you put aside the disparity between boys and girls, and the disadvantage that comes with an impoverished background – Black boys are still doing worse than they should. **According to Ofsted's own figures Black Caribbean pupils are significantly more likely to be permanently excluded from school, and more likely to identified with behaviour related Special Educational Needs.**

"Disproportionate exclusion of Black Caribbean pupils and White and Black Caribbean mixed heritage pupils occurs irrespective of the socio-economic context of the school, its performance, or its educational effectiveness. The results are the same when comparisons are made on the basis of the ethnic compositions of a school, the type of local authority in which it is situated, the percentage of pupils who are entitled to receive free school meals, pupils' attainment and achievement, and standards of pupils behaviour. ...Some schools grade themselves as 'good' and are judged to be good by inspectors even when they exclude a disproportionate number of Black Caribbean heritage pupils."

Ofsted (2008) *Reducing exclusions of Black pupils from secondary schools: examples of good practice.*

Permanent exclusion is the most serious sanction a school can take against a student. While the local authority has a legal duty to make sure that excluded students receive education elsewhere, available evidence indicates that being excluded from school tends to be associated with poor educational outcomes, criminal activity and other forms of antisocial behaviour.

The situation in America is similar where 17% of public school children are African-American, but 41 % of the children placed in 'special ed', and 85% of the time they are African -American male children. A study reported in the Harvard Educational Review in 1987 reported that African American children are placed in 'special ed' more than any other group, stay there for longer, and don't return back to the main classroom on grade level.

Back in Britain Black pupils are also routinely put in bottom sets. According to the **Aiming High Evaluation:** *"whilst many teachers believed setting to be based solely on ability, data indicated that African Caribbean pupils were sometimes relegated to lower sets due to their behaviour, rather than their ability."*

In November 2005, the Department for Education and Skills High Level Group on Race Equality identified exclusions of Black pupils as a priority area for action. This led to a Priority Review to examine the issue in depth entitled ***'Priority Review: Exclusion of Black Pupils "Getting It. Getting it Right." (2006)***. The findings identified concerns about the way the education system treats Black pupils and in particular, the way that a succession of subjective judgements by school staff appear to impact differently on Black pupils.

School exclusions – the facts

Exclusion is an iconic issue within Black communities and is routinely cited by academics as an example of the way the education system discriminates against Black pupils. For Black communities, exclusions are to education what 'stop and search' is to criminal justice. According to the 2006 DfES report every year 1000 Black pupils are permanently excluded and nearly 30,000 receive a fixed period exclusion. Black pupils are three times more likely to be excluded than their white peers, after all other background factors are taken into account. Since 2000 the proportion of Black pupils excluded has increased more rapidly than for any other group. Also Black pupils are less likely to fit the typical profile of excluded White pupils (such as having Special Educational Needs, free school meals, poor attendance records, or criminal records). This evidence challenges the assumption that racial inequalities in education are merely a reflection of socio-economic inequalities in society. It makes a compelling case for the existence of an 'X Factor' related to ethnicity, which explains the exclusions gap. It also supports what academic commentators and Black communities have been saying for over 20 years; that the education system treats Black pupils differently from others. The continued existence of the exclusion gap means that Black pupils are disproportionately denied mainstream education and the improved life chances that go with it.

To make the picture even bleaker, the official statistics underestimate the true level of exclusions among Black boys. The official stats do not take into account the 'informal' or 'back door' exclusions where parents are persuaded to withdraw their child before formal exclusions occur, and many forms of exclusion within school are virtually never recorded. 'Internal exclusions occur in the form of the pupil being subjected to time out both in and outside of the classroom; placed in internal suspension or support units; on extended work-experience; or forced into alternative curricular options.

School exclusions – the causes

A number of theories have been put forward to explain the exclusions crisis. Some commentators focus on in-school factors (policy and practice in schools and the wider education system that produce different exclusion rates for Black and white children despite similar behaviour) whilst others focus on out-of school factors (issues in the wider community which cause Black pupils to behave worse or differently).

One theory, known as **Cultural Dissonance** and put forward in the late 70s argues that white teachers do not understand Black culture and therefore misinterpret the behaviour of Black children and so impose sanctions more frequently and more harshly on Black pupils, leading to conflict and disaffection with school. Whilst some Black pupils are excluded for conduct and behavioural problems, examples of this cultural dissonance would be those pupils excluded for exhibiting culture-specific behaviours such as wearing dreadlocks, braids, having one's hair shaved too short or 'demonstrating inappropriate walking styles'!

Other commentators have sought explanations in the children themselves, arguing that **certain 'racial' groups are intellectually inferior to others** (Jensen 1969; Eysenck 1971; Hernstein and Murray 1994) or that Black children behave more badly and are therefore justifiably placed in lower sets.

The explanation most widely put forward both in Britain and the USA is that **racism** (institutional and individual) has been the main cause of the negative experiences of schooling of Black children. But as with most things in life, the closer you study it, the more complicated it gets. If it is cultural differences or racism that is to blame then why do more recent immigrants or children who emigrate from cultures drastically different from our own, often do better than Black children who come from communities with cultures that are more similar to that of the majority

61

white culture? And why do African-born immigrants do better than those Black children who may be the second or third generation of their family born here?

In school factors
Differential treatment

Nowadays, teachers like most of the rest of society, know that blatant racism will not be tolerated. Openly racist views are deeply unfashionable amongst the middle classes (remember the national outcry over the Jade Goody/Shilpa Shetty racial bullying on *Celebrity Big Brother*?) and most teachers would fight you in the street if you accused them of being racist. Unlike in my school days no modern-day teacher would dare to refer to Black pupils as 'nig-nogs' and 'coons'. Its altogether more subtle - so subtle infact that the teachers themselves may not even be aware of it. It can be manifested in the teachers expectations, either of an exaggeration of threat and violence where there is none, or low expectations of academic ability. According to this school of thought, the exclusions gap is due to institutional racism - decisions made by schools and their staff which have the cumulative effect of producing a racist outcome. This view is supported by the 2006 DfES report which found a compelling case for the existence of institutional racism within schools. The report found that '*whilst*

62

overt racism (at least on the part of the staff) is now unusual, discrimination persists in the form of culturally unrepresentative curricula and low expectations for the attainment and behaviour on the part of staff.'

Black pupils are disciplined more frequently, more harshly and for less serious misbehaviour than other pupils, and such differential treatment is likely to be unwitting on the part of teachers. Slaughter- Defoe and Richards (1994) suggest as early as kindergarten, Black males are treated differently than other male and female students. Throughout elementary and middle school, Black boys are consistently rated lower by teachers for social behaviour and academic expectations (Irvine 1990; Rong 1996).

Black Boys Seen as a threat

This unintentional racism from teachers stems from long standing social conditioning involving negative images of Black people (particularly men), which stereotype them as threatening. Such conditioning is reinforced by the media portrayal of Black street culture. It encourages school staff to expect Black pupils to be worse behaved and to perceive a greater level of threat and challenge in their interactions with Black pupils. Using this analysis, it is possible to explain the statistical evidence that Black pupils are more likely to be excluded for violent incidents. Whether to classify a pupils' actions as 'violent' is necessarily a subjective decision, and such a disproportionality is entirely consistent with perceptions of Black pupils as more threatening.

Majors and Biltson (1994) argue that the demeanours of Black students are misunderstood by White middle class teachers and school administrators as defiant, aggressive, and intimidating. In 1997 Sewell found that not only were Black boys negatively stereotyped by teachers, but also feared by them. He reported that teachers said that they were afraid of Black boys because of their physical size and their views that they were more troublesome than other pupils.

Once again the situation is mirrored in the States.

In chapter one I briefly mentioned **Jawanza Kunjufu** observation in his book, *Countering the Conspiracy to Destroy Black Boys Vol III,* that large numbers of Black females have to go unescorted to the prom because there aren't enough Black boys at High School to go around.

"When you observe the freshman class, you may see numbers that are relatively equal. In typical classes of 600 freshmen, there will be 325 girls and 275 boys. Four years later approximately 300 students will graduate. 200 hundred of those students will be

female and at most a hundred of the student will be male."

The high dropout rate is a result of the disproportionate number of Black males suspended. African American males are 8% of the public school students nationwide, but constitute 37 percent of the suspensions. Numerous studies indicate they are suspended for infractions while other students receive warnings for the same violation.

Black boys seen as lazy and stupid

In 1996 Wrench & Hassan reported that young African Caribbean males felt that teachers often had negative views of them. As Irvine reported, overt and subtle messages are communicated by teachers to pupils about their reliability and ability to succeed and do well.

In addition to the exclusions gap commentators have pointed to numerous examples of where unintentional, systematic discrimination has produced differential outcomes for Black pupils. For example, under the old Baseline Entry tests, Black pupils significantly outperformed their white peers, but when the teacher assessed Foundation Stage Profile replaced these tests, the pattern was reversed. It's hard not to conclude that teachers underrated the ability of Black pupils due to the same subconscious stereotyping of Black pupils that contributes to the exclusion gap.

More recently, in this country in 2008 researchers uncovered evidence that teachers are routinely under-estimating the abilities of some Black pupils, suggesting that assumptions about behavioural problems are overshadowing their academic talents. The survey which tracked 15,000 pupils through their education examined the profile of pupils entered by teachers to take higher tier papers in their maths and science tests at 14. It was found that white pupils were significantly more likely to be entered for the top tiers than their Black Caribbean, Pakistani, Black African and Bangladeshi classmates. For a significant proportion of the Black pupils, there was no academic explanation for them being excluded from the harder papers.

This antipathy regarding the academic achievement of Black boys was testified to by an English and drama teacher of 34 years experience when she spoke to *The Guardian* newspaper in 2008.

"When I first started teaching in 1964 the racism was overt. They sat in staffrooms and said racist things about Black pupils. I didn't know many Black people but I knew what they were saying was wrong. White teachers now know not to be racist, but what happens now is neglect. Its leaving people on their own too long and not being proactive in their development

because you have low expectations, and then asking why they aren't doing enough work.

Although she herself is white, the issue was brought into sharp relief for her when her mixed race son started to take his GCSEs. She fought to get her son entered to take the higher tiered exam papers but the teachers refused.

"Things happened to my youngest (Black) son which never happened to his (white) brothers. At school that was very subtle. No one called to say he wasn't doing his homework. They just didn't expect him to. Nobody follows the kids up if they are falling behind. They just ignored him until he failed. All I know is that my very clever son messed up at school. He got top marks when he left primary school and ended up with three GCSEs. That shouldn't have happened."

A 1999 Ofsted found that teachers' assessments of Blacks were consistently lower than their actual test results. Students with typically African or Asian sounding names were likely to be given up to 12% lower marks in the institutions where anonymous marking was not in place. However Leeds University found that after changing its system to introduce anonymous marking, the scores of Black students rose by 12%.

These racist preconceptions on the part of the teachers has a doubly negative effect. Firstly, because the teacher has little faith in the child's ability she will be unlikely to push him to work harder or enter him for the higher level exams, but secondly, if the child knows that he is generally considered to be intellectually inferior he will indeed perform at a lower level than he might in different circumstances. This effect was beautifully illustrated in 2004 by an experiment by World Bank economists Karla Hoff and Priyanka Pandey. They took 321high caste and 321 low caste 11 - 12 year old boys from rural villages in India, and set them the task of solving mazes. First the boys did the puzzles without being aware of each other's caste, and under this condition the low caste boys did just as well as the high caste boys. Then the experiment was repeated but this time each boy was asked to announce his name, his village and his caste. After this public announcement the boys did more mazes, but this time the performances of the low caste boys dropped significantly. This is striking evidence that performance and behaviour in an educational tasks can be profoundly affected by the way we feel we are seen and judged by others.

Out of School factors

This school of thought argues that Black boys are subjected to influences outside school which cause them to behave less well and/or more aggressively in school. The portrayal of Black men in the popular media, particularly those of the African American ghetto experience and American rap culture which dominates, encourage growing levels of aggression and have encouraged young men to posture aggressively as a means of getting respect. This view is supported by the statistical evidence that **Black pupils are most likely to be excluded 'for violence against a pupil'** (whilst other groups are most likely to be excluded for 'persistent disruptive behaviour') and more likely than average to be excluded for 'violence against a member of staff'.

Another branch of this theory argues that Black boys may be deliberately sabotaging their own success. These pupils do not share the same value system as the school/teachers and by accepting their values (hard work, academic achievement etc.) they will somehow be abandoning their own cultural values. Thus to work hard at school and to speak proper English is to 'act white'. This was a view echoed by the head of the Jamaican Teachers Association **Adolph Cameron** when he visited Britain in October 2011. He argued that some black boys are performing badly on purpose

69

because doing well in school is seen as being feminine, or in the modern vernacular of the youth, being 'gay'.

Ogbu has made an argument that not all minority groups are equal. He separates minority groups into two groups: those in the country voluntarily (immigrant or voluntary minorities) and those that have been subjugated and /or brought into a society against their will. While voluntary migrants may feel grateful to the host country and embrace any opportunities available to them and their offspring, **involuntary minorities** tend to develop a social or collective identity that is in opposition to the social identity of the dominant group. Looking at the American experience voluntary immigrants would be Asian (e.g Indian and Korean) and some Latino (Cuban) populations, whiles examples of involuntary immigrants would be African-Americans, Native Americans and other Latinos (e.g Puerto Rican). Whilst the voluntary immigrants would encourage their children to integrate into mainstream society and embrace its education system as a means to succeed, the children of the involuntary immigrants may be encouraged to value other aspects of society, usually whatever is in opposition to White values.

In Britain we may look on the Windrush generation of Caribbean immigrants in the 50s who came to 'the mother country' full of patriotism and hope, as the voluntary immigrants. Their bitter and rejected offspring may have taken on the oppositional identity of the involuntary group.

Whilst the voluntary migrants may have greater lingual and cultural barriers to overcome than involuntary minority students, they tend to do better because they are able to identify with academia. There is no culture of opposition, no collective identity opposing excelling at school. Gibson and Ogbu found evidence that caste, like minority groups around the world, show poor academic outcomes relative to the majority population, including IQ scores, academic performance, withdrawal from school, and exhibition of behavioural problems. Examples of these groups include: the Maoris of New Zealand, the Baruka of Japan, Oriental Jews in Israel, and West Indians in the UK.

Conclusion

We have seen in this chapter that Black boys are not getting all that they should from their schooling. According to Ofted's report of the 1000 Black pupils who are permanently excluded every year, and the 30,000 who receive a Fixed Period Exclusion, on average these pupils will be one third less likely to achieve 5 GCSEs at A-C grade; be 3 % more likely to be unemployed; experience a reduction of £36,000 in lifetime earnings, be more likely to commit crimes, commit serious crimes and to re-offend; and be more likely to smoke drink and take drugs. Their negative experience of school leaves with them a scar that they will carry with them as they attempt to enter the world of work, and will carry with them for the rest of their lives.

But there is much that parents can do to alter things and the degree of influence of parents on their childrens' academic attainment should not be underestimated. A report by the Joseph Rowntree foundation in 2010 found that young people are more likely to do well at their GCSEs if their parents think it likely that the young person will go onto higher education, spend time sharing family meals and outings, quarrel with their child relatively infrequently, and devote material resources towards education including private tuition and computer and internet access.

(Goodman & Gregg 2010)

Solutions to Problem 2

1 Mothers do not smother your sons. It is said that mothers 'raise their daughters and baby their sons'. We know that this is a mother's natural instinct, but fight against it for his sake. From as early as possible in his development encourage in him a spirit of independence, encourage him to reach each new stage – tie-ing his own shoe laces, making his own bed, making his own breakfast, cleaning up the house, using the washing machine, getting a part time job etc, as soon as he is able. Doing anything else will be stunting his development, and will be hurting him in the long term, not helping him.

2 Carefully consider the choice of school. Don't just send your child to the school nearest your house. Your child's experience at primary school could have repercussions for their whole life. Unless you can afford to send your child to a private school then this really means seriously considering where you are living. When choosing somewhere to live, don't just consider the local shops and the public transport, also consider the local schools. If they are not good enough, then consider living somewhere else. This may sound drastic but this is what white people have been doing for generations. The phenomenon is so common they even have a name for it – they call it

73

'white flight'- white families leaving the racially diverse but economically deprived inner cities in order to enjoy a better quality of life in the suburbs.

According to figures from the Office of National Statistics in 2008 50,000 babies celebrated their first birthday in inner London compared with only 26,000 14 year olds. The pattern is repeated in urban areas in the West Midlands, Liverpool, Cardiff and Greater Manchester. The 20 councils with the lowest average ages of under 16s are in London and Manchester, while the areas with the highest average children's ages are in rural areas of Dorset, Yorkshire, Worcestershire and Cumbria. These ambitious and informed middle class parents are leaving the run down inner cities with their under resourced schools and leaving them to us – but we don't have to stay there either!

3 Keep an eye on your child's friends

As my mother used to say 'if you lay down with dawg, you get flea'.

As EPMD used to rap, 'If you hang with nine broke friends you're bound to be the 10th one'.

Anyone who has parented children past their teens know that once children reach a certain age they stop listening to their parents and pay more attention to their friends. Teenagers don't usually strive to become more like their parents, they strive to impress and fit in with their peers. If their friends have the right values then you've got nothing to worry about. If they are hanging with the wrong company, then you have a problem. Whether they choose to smoke, drink, abuse drugs or run with gangs has much more to do with how their friends behave than with how their parents behave. You want your child to be competing with their friends to see who has got the best grades, not who has got the most expensive trainers or who is the first to lose their virginity. Check out what this year 12 pupil told Ofsted for their 2008 report.

"I was in trouble on and off consistently in the early years of secondary school. I rebelled against school and frequently got into trouble for arguing with teachers. My friends were in even more trouble. In the end they were all excluded and in trouble with the police. I was by myself. I suddenly realised that it was nearly too late for me and I wanted to change."

But don't get depressed thinking that there is nothing that parents can do. You exert a major influence on them by choosing the environment they grow up in. A child is not going to go across town in his pursuit of friends – they are most likely to be his neighbours and his school friends.

4 You must get involved in your child's education.
You can't just send your child to school and hope for the best. If you do that, then clearly it's not the best outcome that will follow. The education process is not just a two way process between your child and the school. It should be a three way dialogue between you, and the school and your child. And that doesn't mean just going to school when your child gets in trouble. Make an effort to get to know the child's teacher right from the start of term, show them that you are onboard and share the same goal – your child's success. Even consider becoming a school governor. Also get involved in your child's homework. If you do this early on and get them into good study habits, then you can leave them to it as they get older and the work gets too complicated for you! (This is especially important for fathers if we don't want our boys to think of academia as something that's feminine or for sissys.) And of course attend every parents evening. Any parent that can't be bothered to attend their child's parents evening frankly has no business raising children.

References for Chapter 2 - Educational Underachievement

Benn, M. and Millar, F. (2006) *A Comprehensive Future: Quality and Equality for all our Children.* London: Compass.

Blair, M. and Bourne, J. (1998). *Making The Difference: Teaching and Learning Strategies in Successful Multi-ethnic Schools.* London. DfEE

Coard, B. (1971) *How the West Indian Child Is Made Educationally Subnormal in the British School System: The Scandal of the Black Child in Schools in Britain.* New Beacon Books Ltd

DfES (2006). *Exclusion of Black Pupils: Priority Review: "Getting It. Getting it Right."*

Gibson, M.A. and Ogbu, J. U (1991) *Minority Status and Schooling: A Comparative Study of Immigrant and Involuntary Minorities,* New York: Garland Publishing.

Goodman, A. & Gregg, P. (2010) *Poorer children's educational attainment: how important are attitudes and behaviour?* York: Joseph Rowntree Foundation.

Hoff, K. and Pandey, P. (2004) *Belief Systems and Durable Inequalities: An Experimental investigation of Indian Caste.* Policy Research Working Paper. Washington D.C. World Bank.

Holland, S. (1989). *Fighting The Epidemic of Failure: A radical strategy for educating inner city boys,'* Teacher Magazine 1, pp. 88-9

Joseph Rowntree Foundation (2005) *Migration and Social Mobility: the life chances of Britain's minority ethnic communities.*

Johnson, S. (2008) 'The Teachers Just Ignored him until he failed.' The Guardian newspaper September 5.

Kunjufu, J. '*Countering the Conspiracy to Destroy Black Boys Vol III'*, Chicago, IL: African American Images.

Majors,R. & Billson, J.M. (1993) *Cool pose : the dilemmas of black manhood in America.* New York : Simon & Schuster.

Ofsted (2008) *Reducing exclusions of Black pupils from secondary schools: examples of good practice.*

Rampton, A. (1981) *West Indian Children in Our Schools.* Cmnd 8273, London: HMSO

Slaughter-Defoe, D. T., & Richards, H. (1995). Literacy as empowerment: The case of African American males. *Literacy among African American youth: Issues in learning, teaching, and schooling*, 125-147.

Swann, Lord (1985) Education for All: Final Report of the Committee of Inquiry into the Education of Children from Ethnic Minority Groups, Cmnd 9453, London HMSO.

Tikly, L. Haynes, J, Caballero, C. Hill, J. (2006) Evaluation of Aiming High: African Caribbean Achievement Project. DfES Research.

Wilson, Gary – (2008) *Help Your Boys Succeed – The Essential Guide for Parents.* Continuum (London)

Wrench, J. Hassan, E, and Owen, D (1996). *Ambition and marginalisation A qualitative study of underachieving young men of Afro-Caribbean origin.* Department for Education and Employment, London (United Kingdom). London : Stationery Office.

PROBLEM 3
Under-employment

Surplus to requirements?

"I went looking for a job everyday last week,
But it turned into a crazy game of hide & seek,
Because everyplace I seemed to look a job wasn't
there,
I might as well apply for food stamps or welfare."
Grandmaster Flash & the Furious Five –
Survival.

Introduction

In the previous chapter we looked at how the education system was failing Black boys. If a child doesn't receive even a basic education, then his chances of success in employment are virtually nil. But in this chapter I will address the fact that even with a high level of educational attainment, young Black men's success in the world of work is far from guaranteed.

In October 2009 the Department of Work and Pensions (DWP) published a report detailing evidence of race discrimination in recruitment procedures. As part of the investigation, the DWP sent out nearly 3,000 job applications to employers in the private, public and voluntary sectors. They found that for every nine applications sent by a white applicant, an equally good applicant with an ethnic minority name had to send 16 to obtain a positive response.

The names that were used for the purposes of this research included: Nazia Mahmood, Muhammed Kahlid, Mariam Namagembe, Anthony Olukayode, Alison Taylor and Andrew Clarke. Details of this survey were published at the time on the **totaljobs.com** website and prompted a flood of responses. One of the most poignant was from a

82

Black job seeker by the name of Tanangui Kwah
detailed below.

See my name and my qualifications - Bsc. Economics,
Msc. Industrial & Financial Economics, Msc.
International Management (Sweden) and Mphil in
Management (Exeter). Diverse work experience in
various companies in Europe and multilingual in
European languages. What do you think I am doing
now? Unemployed now for more that 1 year. I go to
organisations and see lots of incompetent people there
then I ask myself 'what have I done wrong in looking
for work?' Oh! Then it strikes me I am black and I
should have been cleaning or doing some strong
manual labour. Employers prefer to go abroad to the
USA, Canada and Eastern Europe to seek white
people to employ while ignoring highly qualified black
people here. Well, that's how it is and that is how it
will be – nothing will change we black people should
just be intelligent and united enough to start our own
creativity rather than rely on white employers.

Tanangui's frustration is understandable, and his story
is not uncommon. Indeed in my years working as a
health care assistant and mental health support
worker, I worked with many African men who had
degrees in Engineering or Accounting but were
working in healthcare, not because they had any

interest in the profession, but because that was the only area in which they could find employment.

In 2001 Greg Dyke, the then director general of the **BBC** described it as being "hideously white" because of the almost total absence of Black and brown faces within its management structure. I know exactly what he meant. I worked briefly in the **Radio 1** press office in the late 1990s. Despite the fact that at this time Radio 1 was trying to reposition itself and to shake off its 'Smashy and Nicey' image by recruiting specialist DJ's playing R&B, Drum and Bass, and Dancehall Reggae, I was one of only three Black men in the building. The other two were the I.T. man and the security guard on reception! If this was the case at 'cool and trendy' Radio 1 then you can be assured that the situation was even more lily white at the more stuffy Radios 2, 3, and 4.

The situation is the same in **local government.** Research published in 2010 revealed that of London's 33 local authorities, only one (Lambeth) had a non-white chief executive. Even in boroughs that have massive ethnic populations like Newham and Brent the chief executives were still white. The situation is repeated in town halls up and down the country even in multi-racial cities like Manchester, Birmingham, Bradford, Leeds, Liverpool and Bristol.

It may come as no surprise that Black men are struggling to succeed in the corporate world, but even in areas where we are considered to flourish, insiders tell of a different story. One would think that comedy and entertainment is an area where we have always had a presence. In the 70s, even whilst the *Black and White Minstrel Show* was still on television, Black comedian Kenny Lynch was on our screens. In the 80s and the 90s there was Lenny Henry, and in the noughties Richard Blackwood had his own show on Channel 4, not to mention the numerous sketch shows and sitcoms through the years like *No Problem, The Real McCoy,* and *Desmonds*. But for all those individual successes there are scores of Black comedians on the comedy circuit who may be able to fill the Hackney Empire or the Shepherds Bush Town Hall with their shows, but can't get a break onto TV. **Stephen K. Amos,** who got his own show on BBC2 in 2010 revealed the struggle he had before finally getting his shot at the ripe old age of 43.

"About 10 years ago, I had a meeting with an executive who said to me, "you know what, you're really funny, you're ready to make a show right now. But its them" – and he pointed out of the window "-they're not ready for you."

Another producer once said to me: "we really like you but we've just had Richard Blackwood," as if it's one in, one out. I used to do a joke where I said I'd have to wait for Lenny Henry to die before I could get on television. But I can't think of a time when there were two Black performers on any network at the same time. I know lots of comics who've left the country and are trying their hand in American because they feel they're hitting a glass ceiling here."

Exactly the same could be said for Black actors like east London boy Idris Alba who had to find success in the States with the cult TV series *The Wire* before he could get a starring role in this country with the lead role in cop show *Luther*.

But if there is one area of employment that Black men have done well as long as they've been in this country it is in the field of sports. Black players are massively over-represented in the **English football Premier league** (25%), but while they may dominate on the pitch, once they reach the end of their playing careers, they are back to scratching their heads. Whilst the natural progression for a white professional footballer may be to go into coaching or management, that door seems to be closed to Black ex-players. Despite the fact that over a quarter of the players in the Premiership are Black, for much of 2010 there was only one Black man in a management position - Newcastle's Chris Hughton. In an echo of Stephen K. Amos' comment on never seeing more than one Black comedian on the television at a time, shortly after Paul

Ince was awarded a management position at Notts County, Hughton was sacked by Newcastle. That is one man out of 92 clubs in the four top divisions. Throughout most of 2011 there was not a single Black manager in the Premiership.

"Its outrageous, "said former England, Watford and AC Milan striker Luther Blissett in an interview in the Observer newspaper in 2010. "And it does grate with me because I know there are a lot of guys who I played with who would make good coaches and managers, and the opportunity was never afforded them just because of their colour. Some may think that's oversimplifying it, but can you say it's a coincidence when this thing goes on for so long? For the 20 odd years I've been applying for jobs, you start to think to yourself there's got to be more to it than a coincidence."

Despite possessing a Uefa A pro-license coaching qualification, 52 year old Blissett who had a brief spell as a coach at Watford, at the time of the interview was working three days a week at Stevenage with the under 16s, and said he had more or less given up hope of securing a high profile managerial position.

The situation was finally acknowledged by the Professional Footballers' Association in September 2011when it started discussions with Cyrus Mehri, the man who brought 'the Rooney Rule' to the NFL in the

United States. Introduced in 2003 this rule is a form of positive discrimination that demands that Black candidates are at least given an interview when senior coaching positions become available. The step was deemed necessary because in America's NFL, like the English Premier league, though the field of play was dominated by Black players (75%), they were conspicuously absent from managerial positions.

But this is not just a voluntary thing like Britain's own Equality Act of 2010, which allows employers to voluntarily appoint under-represented groups. The Rooney Rule has teeth as the Detroit Lions discovered in 2003 when they were fined £125,000 for not interviewing an African- American for a vacancy. This push brought dividends as by 2010 there were 8 Black coaches in the NFL, and one year the two teams facing each other in the Superbowl were both led by Black coaches. Indeed, according to Mehri, 7 out of 10 of the teams to reach the Superbowl in the following years were led by a Black head coach.

But returning to soccer, in 2010 England bid to host the 2018 World Cup. To support their bid the Football Association sent a top flight delegation including Prime Minister David Cameron, international footballer and fashion icon David Beckham, and heir to the throne Prince William to Zurich to push for votes from the FIFA delegates.

Despite this the bid was unsuccessful, eventually going to Russia. Though FIFA admitted that England had the strongest technical bid, and the best existing infra-structure, they claimed that by allowing nations with a less strong footballing tradition to host the event, they were expanding the horizons and the audience for the sport. Though not even the most patriotic of English men could claim that allowing England to host would expand the audience for what is already the national game and home to the most watched league in the world, what frustrated the F.A. was that they spent so much time and effort in the bidding process, when it had already been decided that the event would be going elsewhere. Why make them waste so much time and energy when they never had any chance of being successful? That feeling of disappointment and frustration is one familiar to many Black men when applying for jobs. They feel that they are qualified and experienced enough to do the job, but feel, like that delegation from the F.A. that they never stood a chance of success.

Those frustrations have haunted many under-employed Black men for generations. But from the boardroom, to our TV screens to the football pitch dugout, just how widespread is the Black man's struggle to find work?

89

Unemployment statistics

Research by the Office of National Statistics published in 2012 found that unemployment rates for 16-24 year olds from and African and African-Caribbean background are double that of white job seekers, with 56% of Black men and 39% of Black women being out of work. The Labour MP Diane Abbott described the figures at the time as an inequality time-bomb.

"It is a fact that Britain's non-white ethnic minorities have lower earnings and much higher unemployment rates being usually at least twice as high as those for white people.   For those that do work, men from minority ethnic groups as a whole are less likely than white men to be in high status or skilled manual occupations, and are more likely to be semi-skilled manual workers."

Centre for Research in Ethnic Relations and Institute for Employment Research (2000)

This fact was even acknowledged by the Prime Minister back in 2003.   In a Cabinet Office report Tony Blair wrote

"Though it is nearly 40 years since the first Race Relations Act, it is clear that racial discrimination in the labour market still persists."

90

Cabinet Office (2003) *Ethnic Minorities and the Labour Market: Final Report.* Strategy Unit, Cabinet Office, London.

Even for the second generation, born and educated in Britain there are significant disadvantages for Black African and Caribbean men in the labour market with respect to unemployment, earnings and occupational attainment. In the government research literature these disadvantages are termed 'ethnic penalties'.

"While the ethnic penalties calculated from statistical models of employment, occupation and earnings must not be equated directly with discrimination, there is considerable evidence from the Home Office Citizenship Survey (HOCS) 2003 and from field experiments that unequal treatment on grounds of race or colour is likely to be a major factor underlying the pattern of ethnic penalties."

Ethnic Penalties in the labour market: Employers and discrimination. **DWP (2006)**

The concentration of ethnic minorities in deprived areas has often been cited as a key cause of high levels of ethnic minority unemployment, however a study by the Department of Work and Pensions in 2006 found that in areas that are predominately white, ethnic minorities are still twice as likely to unemployed than their white counterparts.

91

One quarter of African and Caribbean children live in households in which no adult has a job. For these children, gaining knowledge of how to find jobs and suitable qualifications will not be easy.

Even if these children manage to obtain the right qualifications, their success is still far from assured. As far back as the early 90s studies showed that Black graduates had a harder time finding suitable employment.

Irrespective of their degree or grades, they (Black undergraduates) faced poorer job prospects than their white peers. They made more job applications, faced more rejections, and if fortunate enough to secure employment, generally started at a lower level than their similarly qualified white peers. **(Kirschenman and Neckerman 1991).**

When the economic crisis was just taking hold in 2008, research revealed that white graduates were finding work more easily than their ethnic minority counterparts. They showed that 66% of white graduates found work within a year compared with 56.3% for black, Asian or other ethnic minority students. In 2012 the Higher Education Statistics Authority revealed that Black graduates are 30% less likely to be employed than their white counterparts with just four out of 10 Black students in full time employment six months after leaving university.

Another survey, this time by Warwick University's Institute of Employment Research, tracked 17,000 people from the moment they began applying for a higher education course due to start in 2006 into the winter of 2011-12, gathering information on their views and prospects four times in that period. They also found that non-white graduates are significantly more likely to experience unemployment, while the chance of being in a non-graduate job rises for those whose parents do not have university degrees.

Even those Black people lucky enough to find a job, may still find that they are earning less than their white counterparts.. Researchers from the University of Essex in an article published in the journal *Work, Employment and Society* in 2012 analysed more than 650,000 results from the UK's quarterly Labour Force Survey. This showed that in the four years beginning in 1993, pay per hour for whites averaged £6.90, 40 p more than that earned by Black Caribbeans. By 2008 the gap had closed as more Blacks moved up the corporate ladder, but even where the two groups worked in the same profession, there was a difference in pay. According to Essex University's Malcolm Brynin and Ayse Guveli, by 2008 whites were earning an average of 18p an hour more than non-whites doing the same type of work.

93

"It is clear that on this basis most ethnic minorities earn consistently less than white people," asserted Brynin and Guveli, "if not always by much. One implication is that some minorities do not earn as much as their education would warrant."

The situation is the same in America, where according to the New York Times, the decline in employment since the beginning of the recession in 2008 has been much steeper for Blacks. According to David R. Jones, the C.E.O of the Community Service Society of New York, Blacks were over-represented in fields that suffered the most in the downturn, including government agencies, construction and manufacturing. Jones, who's agency provides services to poor and low-income families told the New York Times that his agency had found that half of the people holding jobs as security guards had batchelor's degrees of had attended college.

Historical Context

It was not always so. Caribbean immigrants coming to Britain in the 50s and 60s were coming to a buoyant labour market, to take up jobs in an expanding economy that had recruited them for jobs for which there was no local competition. The overall employment rate of Caribbeans was quite high in the 1970s – higher infact than that of the white population. But the recession of the early 1980s reduced their prospects to no better than those of whites, and the recession of the early 1990s reduced their rate to well below that of whites. Despite what their parents and grandparents had hoped, prospects for the second and third generation are actually worse than they were for pioneer immigrant generation. Though the overt discrimination may have been less (and by the 90s was unlawful) the economy was very different and the job market much more competitive. In short the immigrant bubble has burst and this once desperately needed foreign workforce were now surplus to requirements. My grandfather told me a story of how he lost his job working on a building site in the 60s, and simply went searching and found another one before the end of the day. This experience stands in stark contrast to his university graduate grandson who took nine months to find a job, some 50 years later. Sadly for Black people when a recession hits, if effects Black people the hardest.

The unemployment rate for young Black men has doubled since the start of the recession in 2008, while among young Blacks overall it has risen by two-thirds to 47.4 %. In contrast just 20.8% of young whites are seeking work, up from15% figures from the Office for Nationals Statistics show. The trend echoes the recession of the early 1990s when unemployment among ethnic minorities rose by 10%, compared with a 6% increase overall.

Gender Differences

But an important caveat must be made. Much research on the extent of the Caribbean penalty has mostly been based on an analysis of unemployment among men. If Black men and women are considered separately it turns out that Black men do indeed have lower employment rates but Black women do not. **Infact Black women have higher employment rates than their white counterparts**, and according to the D.W.P, are the only ethnic minority population who perform better than their white counterparts in the labour market. The reason for this is unclear, but it has long been a source of conflict between Black men and women. 'Why can't you get a job when I always can?' is the accusation Black women have hurled at their unemployed partners for generations. Black women have explained this gender difference as due to Black men's laziness or unwillingness to eat humble pie when in search of a job. Black men may explain it as being due to the discrimination that they face that Black women do not. White male employers, they argue, see Black men as a threat, whereas they don't see Black women in the same light. Whatever the cause, the fact remains that Black women not only fare better than Black men in the jobs market, they fare better than white women too! Sadly this doesn't mean that Black women will be taking over the country any time soon. Whilst Black women may be doing better than their white counterparts, it's a case of having to. Whether they are single mothers or in a relationship, they are often the main breadwinners. There are very few Black women in this country that can afford to be housewives keeping the home fires burning and looking after the children leaving their husbands to 'bring home the bacon'.

Black women have a long history of being employed by the public sector in this country. In the 50s and 60s the NHS was the major employer for females, whilst to the men-folk fell the job of rebuilding the nation after the Blitz. Whilst the semi-skilled manual labour dried up in the 1970s, the health service jobs did not, but the brothers didn't take advantage of it. In the 70s and 80s being a nurse was still not considered a job for a man, and becoming a doctor required a length of study and level of academic achievement that most Black men found prohibitive. Then when Britain's inner cities saw race riots in the early 80s (Brixton, Tottenham and Toxteth), the government increased their efforts to employ more ethnic minorities in local authority jobs. Infact Britain's self proclaimed 'Best Black newspaper' *The Voice,* which launched in the early 80s, built its success on the advertising revenue from the local authorities. To prove that they were serious about employing minorities the local city councils felt duty bound to advertise their vacancies in *the Voice*, and those in the Black community looking for jobs felt duty bound to buy it. But again, for some reason, those who took up the jobs were predominantly the sisters.

This gender difference is also present in the States. In an article entitled **'Plight Deepens for Black Men, Studies Warn'** Baltimore journalist Erick Eckholm reviewed several academic studies on Black employment or the lack of it. *"Black men in the United States face a far more dire situation than is portrayed by common employment and education statistics'* stated Eckholm … *"and it has worsened in recent years even as an economic boom and a welfare overhaul have brought gains to Black women and other groups."*

The share of young Black men without jobs in the States has climbed relentlessly, with only a slight pause during the economic peak of the late 1990s. In 2000, 65% of Black male high school dropouts in their 20s were jobless – that is unable to find work, not seeking it or incarcerated. By 2004, the share had grown to 72% compared with 34% of white and 19% of Hispanic dropouts. Even when high school graduates were included, half of Black men in their 20s were jobless in 2004, up from 46% in 2000.

98

According to federal Labor Department more than half of all African American and other non-Hispanic Blacks in the city of New York who were old enough to work had no job in 2012. One problem, said David R. Jones the president and chief executive of the community Service Society of New York, is that Blacks were over-represented in fields that suffered the most in the downturn, including government agencies, construction and manufacturing.

Comparison with Asian immigrants

As well as the varying degrees of success between Black men and Black women, many have made negative comparisons between immigrants from the Caribbean and those from the Asian subcontinent. 'How is it', they ask, 'that so many Asian immigrants have done so well, either being self-employed or rising up through the medical profession, as Doctors, Dentists, Opticians etc, whilst the Afro-Caribbeans still struggle to make any headway?' Here it is important to make distinction between the origins of these immigrants.

Firstly, it is misleading to lump all those from the Asian subcontinent together in one group. There is a world of difference between the relatively wealthy and educated Indian immigrants who had professional background in business or medicine, and those relatively uneducated immigrants from Pakistan and

Bangladesh. Many of those Indians who were expelled from Kenya or Uganda in the 60s and 70s were already prosperous and successful professionals. When they were uprooted they continued to ply their respective trades and passed the baton to their children.

They were self-reliant entrepreneurs servicing their own communities, not dependent on the white man for a job. When the Ugandan Asians were expelled by Idi Amin in 1972, they were only allowed to take two suitcases and the equivalent of £50 in cash out of the country. (Amin's misguided reasoning for expelling them was that they were bleeding the country dry and not contributing to the economy, and as such he was hardly going to let them take their considerable assets with them.) Though they arrived in Britain virtually penniless, they still had their entrepreneurial spirit and business sense intact. As one Ugandan immigrant supposedly observed to another at the time, "Don't worry doctor, we will become rich here. They close their shops at 5pm!" Once in Britain these Asian-African immigrants built up many successful businesses, and it has been estimated that 30,000 jobs were created by 1000 Ugandan Asian immigrants who settled in Leicester. By 1990 several of these 'poor immigrants' had made it onto the Sunday Times Rich List. They clearly carried with them a very different mind-state than those Caribbean immigrants who came to Britain hoping to eek out a living as 'beasts of burden' working in the Post Office, or on London Transport, or in the NHS.

But whilst the Patels and the Sharmas have thrived in this country, the children of their less well educated Pakistani and Bangladeshi cousins have done far less so. While Indian groups are more likely than any other ethnic group (including whites) to own their own homes, Bangladeshi's have the highest poverty rates of all groups, with almost three quarters of children of Bangladeshi and Pakistani origin living in households below the poverty line..

Whilst Indian and Chinese people tend to have relatively low unemployment rates, Pakistani and Bangladeshi young people are more likely than those from other ethnic groups to be unemployed.

According to the 2001 census, more than a third of Muslim households in Britain had no adults in employment.

As we know the wave of Caribbean immigrants who came in the 50s and 60s came to work on the building sites, in the hospitals and on public transport. They were unskilled, or semi skilled manual labourers. And when the manual labour jobs dried up in the 70s and 80s there was no family business for their children to move into and little advice they could give them to help negotiate a very different job market. Some

Caribbean immigrants did set up their own business of course, but did not seem to enjoy the same success as their Asian counterparts. The influence of growing up in a business orientated family or culture should not be underestimated.

Self Employment/Entrepreneurism – it's not that easy.

For Black men facing discrimination in the job market, setting up your own business seems like a good option. Evidence from the Black Training and Enterprise Council suggests that Black Caribbean and African people are much more likely to consider starting a business, yet only 6% are self-employed or own their own business, compared with 15% of white people. For all those thinking of setting up for themselves, BBC television program *Dragon's Den* should be required viewing. For those who haven't seen it, it is the thinking man's *X Factor,* but with a panel of successful entrepreneurs and business experts replacing the media moguls and record label svengalis, and business start ups looking for investment capital rather than wanna-be pop stars looking for a recording contract. It was on this program that Reggae artists turned Caribbean chef **Levi Roots** won the funding to turn his **Reggae Reggae Sauce** into a nationwide phenomenon.

In one particularly memorable episode the panel of Dragons were greeted by a Black husband and wife couple who had created a range of Caribbean convenience meals. The Dragons enjoyed the food tasting and, as always, proceeded to grill the would-be entrepreneurs about their business' finances. They quickly gleaned that each ready meal cost the couple £1.60 to produce. And guess how much they were selling them to the supermarkets for? £1.60! So it didn't matter how tasty the meals were, or how many units they sold, this business would never make a profit. It was not apparent if the couple realised this before entering the Den, but once this fact was revealed they hung their heads with embarrassment and shame. The wife even started to cry and tried to blame it on her husband. 'He's no good at maths' she said, 'I told him.' Which made me wonder, if you know he's no good at maths why did you allow him to make the business decisions? Naturally, most of the Dragons recoiled at the idea of investing in a business which could not turn a profit run by two people with such an obvious lack of business acumen, but one of the Dragons took pity on them. James Caan, the multi-millionaire Asian businessman explained that he knew a lot about this market, as his sister already ran a similar business selling Asian ready meals to supermarkets, and he correctly observed that they had already done all the hard work by designing a range of meals, and getting them into the shops. All the business needed to get it working was to change their distribution deal and bring down their manufacturing costs. The couple eventually got the money they were looking for, in return for a 50% share of their business. I personally thought that the Dragons should have taken a 100% share of the business and let the couple work for them, as they clearly had no business sense! What this tale nicely illustrates is that there is a big difference between being a good cook and running a successful catering business, just like there is a big difference between enjoying looking after other peoples' children and running a successful day care centre or nursery. That difference is business acumen, and it,s not something most people are naturally born with – you have to learn it. And where do you learn it from? To illustrate let me tell you another story.

In 2008 my grandmother died at the age of 90. It just so happens that at that time the youngest child of an Asian family who lived across the road from my grandmother's house was a pupil in the class that my wife taught. When the boy saw my wife in class he politely offered his condolences, but what he said next shocked my wife. He asked if the family would be interested in selling the house! At only 10 years of age this boy had already grasped the concept of 'a motivated seller', something that I did not learn about until in my 30s at an expensive business seminar designed to help budding millionaire landlords expand their property portfolio. 'A motivated seller' is someone who is selling their house and for some reason is so eager for a quick sale, that they will accept less than the market value. People such as a divorced couple who can no longer stand the sight of each other and are desperate to go their separate ways, or the children of a deceased parent for whom all proceeds will be clear profit, and are eager to sell so that they can divide up the proceeds between themselves. This ten year old understood this because his family already owned several properties.

You can often see such other young entrepreneurs-in-training when you go to your local Asian corner shop, where you will often see a child who looks barely old enough to be in secondary school working the till. When in 8 or 10 years time these young men are ready to go into business themselves, they will already have a decade's worth of on-the-job experience and numerous family members willing to invest and lend support - two things that very few Black folks have. Thus it came as no surprise to me that the 2010 winner of the BBC's Junior Apprentice reality game show was Asian teenager Arjun Rajyagor.

It is important to understand that these apparent racial differences are due to culture not race, as illustrated in

1983 by an American sociologist, who compared the understanding of basic economics between children of two different cultures. **Jahoda** showed that 9 year olds in Harare, Zimbabwe, had more advanced understanding of economic principles than British 9 year olds. The Harare children, who were involved in their parents' small business, had a strong motivation to understand the principles of profit and loss. Jahoda set up a mock shop and played a shopping game with the children. The British 9 year olds could not explain about the functioning of a shop, did not understand that a shop keeper buys for less than he sells, and did not know that some of the profit has to be set aside for the purchase of new goods. The Harare children, by contrast, had mastered the concepts of profit and understood about trading strategies. They were not more intelligent than the British children but had grasped these abstract principles as a direct result of their own active participation in the running of a business.

As any watcher of *Dragon's Den* knows, just because you have a good idea and a passion for it, doesn't mean you have a successful business.

The Black work ethic

In his excellent book *Outliers,* author **Malcolm Gladwell** explores our ideas about success. He argues that we all too often buy into the myth that these

106

people are 'self made men' gifted with genius or an incredible work ethic or simply a God-given talent that allows them to be more successful than their peers. But in *Outliers* Gladwell explodes this myth. He argues that no-one makes it by themselves. He shows everyone from Canadian ice hockey players, to Jewish lawyers in New York, to IT millionaires like Bill Gates owe their success to being born in the right place at the right time, and being able to take advantage of a unique set of circumstances.

"*Success is not a random act. It arises out of a predictable and powerful set of circumstances and opportunities," argues* **Gladwell**.

In discussing the economic success of the descendants of American immigrants he assesses how in the space of three generations Jewish immigrants went from being Tailors, garment makers, and leather tanners to Lawyers and Doctors.

"*Jewish doctors and lawyers did not become professionals in spite of their humble origins. They became professionals because of their humble origins*" (Gladwell 2008 p 153)

It has been a source of debate why immigrants who came to America many generations after the African Americans, within a few generations can rise up the ladder of success, leaving those African Americans who arrived before them behind. A similar situation has happened in Britain with the varying success of West Indian and Asian immigrants. By way of explanation of the success of the Jewish immigrants Gladwell introduces the concept of *'meaningful work.'*

"Those three things – autonomy, complexity, and a connection between effort and reward – are most people agree the three qualities that work has to have if it is to be satisfying. Hard work is a prison sentence if it does not have meaning."
(Gladwell 2008 p 149)

These Jewish and Eastern European immigrants to America in the early part of the 20th century, may have been dirt poor, without even a mastery of the country's language, but they developed skills and attitude that would be an invaluable lesson for their children. Those involved in meaningful work are engaged and challenged by their work, and most importantly, those who are self employed can see the relationship between effort and reward, an invaluable lesson to pass onto their children. That is a lesson that those immigrants who are simply involved in manual labour working for someone else cannot pass onto their children.   Gladwell makes the same link to Chinese workers in the paddy fields.

"Throughout history the people who grow rice have always worked harder than almost any other kind of farmer. Working in a rice field is ten to twenty times more labour-intensive than working on an equivalent size corn or wheat field. What redeemed the life of a rice farmer however was the nature of that work.   It was a lot like the garment work done by Jewish immigrants to New York. It was meaningful."
(Gladwell 2008 p 236)

Gladwell argues that this culture of rice farming has imbued in people of Asian decent a powerful work ethic that is evident from the following Chinese proverbs.
'In winter the lazy man freezes to death."
'Don't depend on heaven for food, but on your own two hands carrying the load."
No one who can rise before dawn three hundred and sixty days a year fails to make his family rich."
Compare the meaningful work enjoyed by Chinese paddy field workers and Jewish and Eastern European immigrants to America, with the experience of Black sharecroppers in American's south as described by James Q Wilson in his article *Slavery and the Black Family*.

109

"..after the end of slavery, there was little land available for Blacks to purchase; instead Black men could work land owned by other men and get a share of the crops as their reward. Sharecropping made Black men into marginal members of society who were rewarded not by profits earned from land but for labor extracted from their families. Sharecropping provided an incentive to have a lot of children but no incentive to educate them. And since the land children farmed was not owned by their fathers, the labor never led anywhere."

Hardly what you would call meaningful work. And Gladwell argues that this Asian work ethic has continued into education.

'Go to any Western college campus,' he argues, 'and you'll find that Asian students have a reputation for being in the library long after everyone else has left.'

In my own experience at University in the late 80s there was a noticeable difference between the African students and the Afro-Caribbean/ Black-British ones. The African students were not interested in joining the African Caribbean Society and socialising in the Student Union bar. They were at university for one thing and one thing only – to study. Unfortunately for many of us Afro-Caribbean students (myself included) the studying was the thing that got in the way of a good rave. I noticed the difference again many years later in the late 90s when I worked for a short time at Wormwood Scrubs prison in West London. Whilst working in the education department I discovered the great over-representation of Black inmates (more about that in Chapter 4). These Black inmates were Black British, or fresh from Jamaica, or from Africa (the latter two groups tended to be drugs mules). For a few months I taught all of these groups as well as the indigenous white population, but there was a noticeable difference in the attitude between the foreigners and the British. The Africans lapped up the classes. They were model students doing their homework assignments and eager for more. The British ones on the other hand (both white and Black) seemed only to be there to get out of doing something more demeaning, or as a way of getting out of their cells for a couple of hours. They often didn't do their homework and rarely completed the courses.

Could it be that those generations that languished in slavery, without any automony, who came to view work as oppression, the blood and sweat of their labour not benefiting them but only their oppressors, came to view work as a curse, as something to hate and to avoid? For some present day anecdotal evidence go to any Caribbean takeaway and you won't find any staff who seem happy to be there.

Compare and contrast that with the very different attitude from that displayed in Chinese or an Indian takeaway.

Level playing field?

We are sold the myth that through hard work and the sweat of our brows we can be anything we want to be – reach the top echelons of society. It is feeding everyone this dream that fuels the capitalist machine and keeps society ticking over. The Windrush generation of immigrants worked hard in menial jobs in the hope that their children would do better. Their children, the second generation, had the advantage of being born here, and receiving an English education. If we could take this English education and manage to make it to University then the sky would be the limit; there would be no stopping us – or so our parents' generation believed. Unfortunately any of my generation who bought into that dream found that when we left university, it wasn't quite as simple as that.

"It is very important to recognise that ethnic minorities' difficulties in obtaining employment are not restricted to those with low levels of education and training. Ethnic minorities face difficulties in gaining employment regardless of their level of education."

Ethnic Penalties in the labour market: Employers and discrimination. **DWP (2006)**

It is not just Black people who face these difficulties. While Chinese boys are among the highest-performing groups in schools, figures show that they can expect to earn 25% less than white graduates. Going to the local average comprehensive school, even if you were a hard worker and reasonably intelligent, would result in average GCSEs and A levels (3 As seem to be average these days!!) If you were motivated you could turn these average A levels into a place at an average university. But on graduation and entering the job market you are competing with people who's education was anything but average. What people who are not in-the-know (i.e parents who haven't been to university) don't realise, but those who are in the know (i.e employers who have been to university) do realise, is that there is a vast difference between the level of education received whilst attending one of the country's top universities and one of the average ones.

"There are important differences in the benefits of degrees once graduates leave university, and these tend to work to the disadvantage of non-white people. The institution attended, the choice of subject, level of attainment and route into university all influence how

valuable a degree is perceived by employers."
(Ramsey, 2008)

What I and my mother didn't realise when I was applying to universities aged 18, but those who come from families who have studied at Higher Education level do, is that there is a hierarchy/league table of universities. Firstly between the newer universities (ex-polytechnics) and the older ones; then amongst the old universities there is the more prestigious Russell Group (the top 20), and then within the Russell group there is most prestigious Oxford and Cambridge. (Even within Oxford there is the exclusive Bullingdon club, that is open only to children of the aristocracy and the super-rich). A media studies degree from an ex-polytechnic will not be viewed the same as Politics, Philosophy and Law from Oxford, even though they are both university degrees.

This was brought vividly home to me in 2011 when I went to a reunion of my former colleagues from *The Voice* newspaper. The careers of journalists who made their start at *The Voice,* or any other publication in the 'Black media' for that matter, tend to evolve in one of three ways.

1. They successfully crossover into the mainstream, landing a job at the BBC or on Fleet Street (which is what I tried and failed to do).

114

2. They continue to eek out a living from the meagre pickings in the Black press.

3. They leave the media all together and change careers (which is what I ended up doing).

Whilst at the Voice reunion, I realised that the way former colleagues careers turned out seemed to have little to do with them as individuals, and more to do with their university education. Those of my former colleagues who successfully crossed-over were quite often 'Oxbridge' graduates. Our experience at *the Voice* counted for little in the mainstream job market, but that Oxbridge degree sure counted for something. It's not a guarantee of success - obviously talent and the right attitude are important - but it certainly doesn't hurt!

A study by the National Union of Students and HSBC released in **2009** shows that there are vast differences between the amount of contact time that students have with their lecturers depending on which course they are studying, at which university, ranging from 22.6 hours a week for those studying medicine and dentistry to less than nine hours for those doing subjects such as languages, history and philosophy. Those at the most prestigious universities receive significantly more time with academics through lectures, individual tutorials and drop in sessions than those at other institutions.

Part of the reason that Black university graduates don't fare as well as their white counterparts in the job market is that Black students are less likely to go to the elite universities.

Much of the talk about ethnic minority graduates has focused on Oxbridge, mostly because of its staggeringly low acceptance rate for black students. After issuing a freedom of information request that helped shed light on the Oxbridge situation, the MP David Lammy wrote:

"Universities are not like supermarkets: their job is to serve the country, not just the customers who happen to walk through their doors." Those doors are a lot harder to get through if you aren't white."

A 2012 study by the Black employment charity Elevation Networks and the think-tank the Bow Group cited statistics showing that 46% of Black students who came from London stayed in the city to study for their degree, compared with just 3% of white students who grew up in the capital. In 2012 there were almost as many black students attending London Metropolitan University as in the entire Russell Group. The reasons for this are multiple. Poorer 'A' level results and racism on the part of universities in their admission process may be contributory factors, but probably more important is the fact that often Black students are the first in their families to go to university, and so do not have the knowledge of parents and older siblings to guide them through the selection and application process. Not only that, but since Black undergraduates are twice as likely to come from poorer households then they would probably not want to suffer the greater debt incurred by living away from home on-top of their spiralling tuition fees. In a recession when there is a surplus of available labour, employers are spoilt for choice and may not even bother looking beyond graduates from the elite universities, thus leaving the Black graduates out in the cold.

It's not what you know.........

A truly depressing fact for graduates from poorer backgrounds is that, even if they work hard at school and get to a 'good university', and work hard there and get a 'good degree', they are still not on an equal footing with their competitors in the job market who went to fee-paying schools. A study by Bristol University found that just 58% of state-school educated graduates found a professional job, compared to 74% of independently educated graduates in the same period. Of those students who secure a graduate job, their starting salaries are between £2000 and £3000 lower than their peers who were educated within the fee paying sector. The figures from a report by upReach, a charitable initiative launched in January 2013 to help students from the least affluent backgrounds reach their potential, suggests that the financial returns on higher education are not the same for all graduates. Its not just the quality of education that you receive at these establishments, its the people you meet and the friends you make whilst there, who will be in a position to help you later in life. The students at these elite universities are the future leaders and captains of industry. One of my former colleagues at *the Voice*, who went on to work at *the Guardian* also went to Oxford, and happened to be there at the same time as Chelsea Clinton, the daughter of Bill, former President of the United States. (Those are the kind of contacts that money can't buy). And it can't just be a co-incidence that at the start of this decade, three of the most powerful men in British politics, Prime Minister David Cameron, the chancellor of the exchequer George Osborne, and the Mayor of London Boris Johnson all went to Oxford and are all former members of the afore mentioned Bullingdon club.

A bright student from an impoverished background, who hoped to repay their scholarship to an elite University by locking themselves away in the library and studying all day and all night, would not gain the same benefits from their time there, as a more

118

affluent, more socially confident student who was also able to take advantage of the social and networking opportunities available during their higher learning.

In early **2008** the then Labour government released a white paper looking at the obstacles to careers such as law, medicine and the media, including the role of informal networks used by middle class parents to get their children a head start through work experience or internships.

Government figures show more than two thirds of leading barristers and 9 out of 10 of the most senior army officers are still privately educated, whilst students applying to study medicine or dentistry are twice as likely as applicants for other subjects to be children of professionals. Increasingly the first step in building a career is to secure work experience, often via placements that go unadvertised.

Heather McGregor is a columnist for the Weekend Financial Times as well as running her own executive search business. She believes that the real barrier to social mobility is not the abolition of the grammar schools or the introduction of university tuition fees, but rather the growth of these unpaid internships and work experience placements through which thousands of school and university students gain valuble experience of the workplace.

119

"I mean the thousands of work experience placements and internships, almost all of them unpaid, which well-connected parents who are able to support their children working for nothing are able to arrange," she wrote in the Observer newspaper. "These give already privileged youngsters a head start on their career, while making the playing field even more uneven for others."

The coalition government attempted to address this in 2011, when the then deputy Prime Minster Nick Clegg, unveiled a social mobility strategy that urged firms to give more youngsters a chance of valuable work experience by offering internships "openly and transparently" and providing cash support in the form of at least the minimum wage or reasonable expenses. Mr Clegg said, "career chances should not be decided by "who your father's friends are" and that internships had wrongly been the preserve of "sharp-elbowed'' rich families with contacts and money". Fine words, but the great irony of this was that Mr Clegg himself secured his first internship before going to Cambridge University, when his bank boss father Nicholas "had a word" with a friend at a - Finnish bank. He later got the break which launched his political career when family friend Lord Carrington recommended him to ex-minister Sir Leon Brittan, then Britain's Conservative EU

Commissioner   in   Brussels.

If you're a lucky enough to have a father with powerful friends like Nick Clegg, even after securing one of these invaluable unadvertised work placements, it's highly likely that your entry level job will go unadvertised too. A report released by the **Social Market Foundation in 2010** found that informal recruitment through word of mouth is particularly prevalent in the creative industries such as advertising, architecture, design, publishing and journalism. "Contacts are very important for getting into the sector," claimed Ryan Shorthouse, a social policy researcher and editor of the report *'Disconnected: Social Mobility and the Creative Industries"* ., because word-of-mouth recruitment is more common than formal recruitment methods.

These hidden ladders are more likely to be seized by the children of the professional classes, kept informed by the friends and contacts of their parents. An average degree received from an average university by the child of working class parents does still not give a Black child access to this network. Far from moving up the career ladder, too many Black men can't even get a foot on it.

Solutions

1 What do want to be when you grow up?

Encourage your children to start thinking about what career they would like to pursue as early as possible. If they wait until they have finished school or university they will already be behind. In 2009 the Labour government acknowledge this by announcing a government strategy to give children as young as 10, careers advice. Ed Balls, the then secretary of state for children schools and families admitted that radical change was needed.

"We know its often too late for children to start thinking about this at 14, when they are influenced from when they are seven, eight and nine."

Children don't really understand the job market, other than those jobs they see on TV such as policeman, fireman, footballer, pop star etc., so you're going to have to prompt their thinking. Look at their talents and aptitudes. If they like music encourage them to think about being a musician or producer or songwriter rather than just the artist on stage. If they like reading books then how about considering being an author or playwright? If they like cars, then why not think about designing them rather than just aspiring to drive them or fix them? If they like sport then what about being a coach, a sports psychologist, or a sports journalists rather than just the dumb athlete? You get the idea.

2 Closely monitor changes in the job market.

The jobs market like the economy is constantly changing. An area where there might have been a chronic shortage at one time may be overflowing with job seekers, or have dried up completely some years later. Look how the internet has decimated some previously buoyant industries. Many newspapers are now struggling for survival because of the changing way people now get their news, and record shops have all but disappeared from our high streets. In short the career your child chooses aged 12 may no longer be a viable proposition at 16. As I write, there is apparently a chronic shortage of science graduates from university. In 2009 it was reported that in order to drag the UK out of recession almost 6000,000 engineers would need to be recruited and trained over the next seven years. If you're about to go to university now, then a degree in maths, physics, chemistry or engineering may well enhance your job prospects, but that may not still be the case in ten years time.

3 Its not what you know, it's who you know.

Contrary to what the pioneer generation believed, a good education is not all you need to get a good job. You need qualifications, experience and contacts, and you should try and get all of these at the same time. We know how you get qualifications, but how do you get experience and contacts? Well the easiest way is to work for free. Working for free at the age of 21 after you've just graduated from university and are deeply in debt may be a big ask, but is easier if your still in your teens and living at home. Once they've identified what area they'd like to work in, then both of you can try and make contact with a company working in that area and attempt to get a work placement. If successful then it can serve a dual purpose – firstly to see the industry up close and help them decide if it is really for them, and secondly if it is for them it helps to make contacts and increase the chances of getting a job further down the line. People will always rather employ someone they already know.

4 Work for someone else before you start out on your own.

Being self-employed is a laudable ambition, but don't jump straight into it after leaving school. Whatever area you wish to start business in, get a job working for someone else in that field first. Firstly it will give invaluable insider knowledge from the other side of the counter, and secondly will build up essential contacts and maybe even future customers/clients.

5 Consider moving to where the jobs are.

Remember that Black people, as the descendants of immigrants, are only in this country because our parents or grandparents moved here for the work. If the work has dried up here, then maybe it's time to move somewhere else where the opportunities are more plentiful. You may not like the idea of your children emigrating, but wouldn't you rather visit them in Australia than in jail?

References for Chapter 3 - Under employment

Cabinet Office (2003) *Ethnic Minorities and the Labour Market: Final Report.* Strategy Unit, Cabinet Office, London

Centre for Research in Ethnic Relations and Institute for Employment Research (2000)- *Minority ethnic participation and achievements in education training and the labour market.* University of Warwick.

Department for Work and Pensions (2006) *Ethnic Penalties in the labour market: Employers and discrimination.*

Department for Work and Pensions (2006) *Ethnic Minority Populations and the labour market: an analysis of the 1991 and 2001 Census* (2006)

Gladwell, M. (2008) *Outliers – The Story of Success.* Penguin Books (London)

Jahoda, G. (1983) *European lag in the development of an economic concept: a study in Zimbabwe.* British Journal of Developmental Psychology. 1983, vol. 1, n°2, pp. 113-120

Kirschenman, J and Neckerman, K.M. (1991) *Hiring strategies, racial bias and inner city workers*. Social Problems 433 (1991)

McGeehan P. 'Blacks miss out on jobs rebound in New York City'. The New York Times (20/6/2012)

McGregor H. 'This will never be a fair country while middle class children get all the perks." The Observer 27/02/2011

Ramsey, A. (2008). *Graduate earnings: an economic analysis of returns, inequality and deprivation across the UK.* Belfast: Department for Employment and Learning, Northern Ireland.

The Social Market Foundation (2010). *'Disconnected: Social Mobility and the Creative Industries*

Wadsworth & Wilson (2010) *"Hideously white? The great racial divide in top jobs at town halls."* The Guardian newspaper. October 11th

PROBLEM 4
CRIME
Dying for respect?

"Talk about Justice, and how little we get,
Yet Black men be killing Black men for talking shit!"
Masta Ace

"Where justice is denied, where poverty is enforced,
where ignorance prevails and where one class is made
to feel that society is in an organised conspiracy to
oppress, rob and degrade them, neither persons nor
property will be safe."
Frederick Douglas, 1866

Introduction

On November 27, 2000, ten year-old Damilola Taylor finished school and set off for a computer club meeting at his local library. CCTV cameras recorded him bouncing and skipping along in his distinctive silver Puffa jacket without a care in the world. At around 4.45pm he began his walk home to St Briavel's Court on the North Peckham Estate where his mother Gloria was waiting with his dinner. Damilola, who was brought up in Nigeria, had only arrived in Britain with his family three months earlier. The Taylors believed a new life in Britain would help their daughter Gbemi get treatment for a severe form of epilepsy. Damilola hoped to become a doctor and discover a cure for his sister's condition. But Damilola never made it home that evening. Nobody witnessed the attack which took his life or heard any sound of a struggle or cry for help. All that remained was a trail of blood which carpenter Guillermo 'Bill' Casal followed to a stairwell in Blake's Road, Peckham. He climbed the steps to the second floor and found Damilola slumped against a wall with blood pouring from his thigh. Asked what happened, Damilola could only reply: 'I'm OK, I'm OK.'. Damilola had been stabbed in the thigh just above his knee and bled to death from an injury to his femoral artery. As a murder investigation got underway, Damilola's mother revealed that her son had complained of being bullied two days earlier. Gloria Taylor said in a statement: 'Damilola had been in a fight. He told me that boys at school had been beating him and his arms and shoulders hurt.' She had visited the school just hours before his death to meet the Headmaster to discuss the claims but was reassured it was only a 'low-level problem.' Mrs Taylor told police: 'Damilola used to take only his schoolwork and drawings to school. I never gave him pocket money so he wouldn't have had any with him. 'He didn't have any jewellery, not even a watch. Nor did he carry any valuables like a Walkman or mobile phone. I didn't have enough money for these sort of things.' The only thing that may have attracted the attention of the killers was his silver Puffa jacket of which he was so proud. Police officers had also discovered the broken pieces of a glass beer bottle at the start of the blood trail. These were later reconstructed in the laboratory and a dagger-like shard was confirmed as the most likely murder weapon. A post-mortem examination also revealed a glass marble was lodged in Damilola's throat.

Although detectives investigating Damilola's death hit a wall of silence in the community, the team were given several names by youths in the Peckham area. Rumours had spread that a notorious local gang known as the 'Younger Younger Peckham Boys' were responsible. The group was known to menace the area, mugging younger boys for their valuables and pocket money.

Four youths were tried and acquitted of Damilola's murder in 2002. Three other youths were cleared of murder after a second trial at the Old Bailey in 2006. One was cleared on all charges but the jury failed to reach a verdict on a charge of manslaughter against the other two, brothers Danny and Rickie Preddie, aged 18 and 19. After a 33-day re-trial the brothers were convicted and in October 2006 they were sentenced to eight years' youth custody for the manslaughter of Damilola. They were just 12 and 13 years old when they committed the crime.

Of all the problems that this book covers, none gets greater coverage than Black men and crime. You tend not to see too many documentaries on Black family breakdown, or school exclusions, or mental illness, but hardly a month will pass without some major news story of Black men involved in a stabbing, or a shooting, or the problem of street gangs, or gang rape or the knife crime epidemic. And the nature of this problem, more than any of the others covered in this book, has changed most drastically in the last generation. Unstable families have been part of the Black experience since slavery; under-employment became a problem when recession hit Britain in the 1970s; and educational underachievement and mental illness became a feature of Black lives as soon as second generation immigrants faced institutional racism within the British system. But when we came to this country on mass in the 1950s the violent attacks we had to worry about came from racist Teddy boys, and then from Skinheads and the National Front in the 70s. Now the greatest threat to our safety comes from people who look just like us.

Reasons why Black men should be over-represented within the criminal justice system can be quite easily explained – unstable families and impoverished backgrounds lead to underachievement in schools, social exclusion and a lack of job prospects, until a life of crime seems the only viable career option. These societal factors coupled with the racist preconceptions of those charged with enforcing the law, easily leads to the over-representation in the country's penal system. Naturally members of rival criminal gangs will be involved in competition over territory which may spill over into violence, but the motivation of recent youth violence often seems motivated by little more than a dirty look or a postcode. Why Black boys should be murdering other Black boys who look just like them in such numbers, and why they would be raping Black girls who look just like their sisters and show no remorse, no empathy for their brethren or sistren, is harder to fathom. I will attempt to explain both of these processes in this chapter.

Black on Black Crime

The Notting Hill Riots in the 1950s were a response to the racist attacks from white thugs.

The social uprisings in Brixton, Tottenham and Toxteth in the 80's were a response to heavy-handed and discriminatory Police targeting of Blacks. The biggest 'race stories' of the 90s were the racially motivated murders of Black teenagers of Roland Adams and Stephen Lawrence. But the naughties saw a definite sea change.

In 2000 **Damiola Taylor** bled to death on a stairwell in Peckham after being stabbed in the leg by two other Black teenagers.

In 2003 **Letisha Shakespeare and Charlene Ellis** were killed in the crossfire of rival gangs whilst attending a New Year's eve party.

In 2005 a young Black mother at a christening party was shot dead by a gang of teenage armed robbers in a community centre in Peckham.

In 2006 **Jesse James** was another innocent victim of gang violence in Moss Side Manchester.

2007 was a particularly bad year.

In February, three Black teenagers were shot and killed in 11 days in south London.

In March two Black schoolboys were stabbed to death in London in the space of six days.

Carlos Cyrus was just 12 years old in 2007 when he and 20 teenage gang members stabbed 22 year old pharmacy student **Yasin Abdirahman** to death, mistaking him for someone else.

And it's not just the boys – Black girls are getting in on the murderous act as well, as illustrated by this chilling story from July 2008. Samantha Joseph was 15 when she lured love struck 16 year old **Shakilus Townsend** to a quiet cul-de-sac in south London where he was beaten with baseball bats and stabbed six times by a gang who's leader, Danny McLean, was her ex-boyfriend who she was trying to win back.

On April 14th 2010, 16 year old school girl **Agnes Sina-Inakoju** was shot dead as she waited in the queue at a fast food restaurant in Hackney. Unlucky Agnes just happened to be in the wrong place at the wrong time. The gun shots were apparently aimed at a boy who was also in the takeaway, in retaliation for a street fight that he had been involved in earlier.

The very next month a 15 year old schoolboy was stabbed to death outside of his school. **Zac Olumegbon** from Brixton Hill, south London, and a friend were ambushed by four young men at the gates of Park Campus school in nearby West Norwood.

135

In 2011 we only had to wait three months for the first innocent child to be gunned down. On March 29th **Thusha Kamaleswaran** became the youngest ever victim of gang violence when the five year old girl was shot in the chest and a 35 year old man shot in the face by teenagers on bicycles who chased two youths into a shop in Stockwell Road, south London and opened fire indiscriminately. Luckily her 12 year old brother and three year old sister who were in the shop with her at the time were unhurt. An 18 year old, a 17 year old and a 14 year old were all later arrested.

These are just the horrific headline-grabbing stories of the innocents caught in the crossfire. The murders of one gang member by a rival do not even make the news any more, or as one tabloid journalist put it in the 2005 book **_Guns & Gangs,_** _"Its very frustrating because there are often very good stories behind these incidents, but my news desk is just not interested. To stand a chance of getting into the paper these murders and court cases have to involve either two people being shot, a child, or an innocent passer-by, who's preferably white."_ (McLagan 2005)

Some of these murder scenes were documented by photo-journalist **Antonio Olmos**. In 2011 he embarked on a project to take pictures at every murder scene in London throughout the year. After seven months into it he made this observation.

"I have been struck by the correlation between London's most economically deprived areas – its east and south – and the murder trail that I have followed. Struck too, by how many of the dead young men caught up in gang violence have been of Afro-Caribbean origin. Most depressing of all is the knowledge that most of these young men are part of what I fear is a growing under-class, failed by both education and their parents, part of a lost youth who lives and deaths are largely invisible."

In the three year period ending in 2003-04, 31% of Black homicide victims were shot compared with just 6% of white people. Figures from the now defunct **Operation Trident,** a Metropolitan Police Service (MPS) operation set up to combat shootings among Black Londoners, show that of all MPS firearms homicides and shootings in 2006, **75% of victims and 79% of suspects were Black.** The peak age for victims and suspects of Trident murders and shootings was 19. Figures provided to the inquiry by the Mayor of London show that Black people in London are **7 times more likely than white people to be the victim of homicide,** three times more likely to be domestic violence victims, three times more likely to be raped, and 2.6 times more likely to suffer violent crime.

The Crime Stats

If we relied solely on the news for our information we would get the impression that all Black youth were running rampant on the streets killing at will. The truth of course is very different. Government statistics show that 85% of young arrestees are white, 6% are Black and 3% are Asian. **(source: Home Office Statistics on Race and the Criminal Justice System - 2005).**

But we are still wildly overrepresented when we remember that Black people are less than 3% of the population of this country.

Young Black people represent fewer than 3% of all 10-17 year olds but constitute **6% of those within the youth justice system**. In 2005 Trevor Phillips the Chair of the now defunct Commission for Racial Equality warned that there were twice as many Black boys in prison as university. Evidence from the Home Office's Offending Crime and Justice survey in 2003 found that white males aged 10-25 were far more likely to have committed an offence within the last year than young males in other groups (28% compared with a range of 12% to 19% for other ethnic groups). But the survey found that once young Black people committed an offence, they were more likely to come to the attention of the police. Black people of all ages **are three times more likely to be arrested than white people, six times more likely to be arrested**

for drug offences, 11 times more likely to be imprisoned, and are up to 26 times more likely to be stopped and searched than their white counterparts and twice as likely to be on **the national DNA database.**

According to figures obtained in 2009 by the campaign group Genewatch, almost 45,000 Black children aged 10 – 17 in England and Wales (about 23% of all Black children in the age group) had been added to the database in the previous five years. By contrast that's compared to 10% of white children aged 10 – 17. In the House of Commons Home Affairs Committee report *Young Black People and the Criminal Justice System* (2007) Baroness Scotland confirmed that three quarters of the young Black male population will soon be on the DNA database.

Whereas Black young offenders accounted for **6% of total offences in 2004-05 they received 11.6% of total custodial sentences.**

But before a Black child has committed any crime, his relationship with Police may be soured by the negative, intrusive and humiliating practice of 'stop and search.' Analysis by the London School of Economics and the Open Society Justice Initiative found that there are 41.6 Section 60 searches for every 1,000 white people – making Black people 26.6 times more likely to be stopped and searched, according to the analysis of Ministry of Justice figures for 2008-09.

139

In London, home to more than two thirds of Black people in England and Wales overall, young Black Londoners aged under 18 make up 15% of the population of that age-group but represent 37% of those stopped and searched,

31% of those accused of committing a crime,

26% of pre-court decisions,

49% of remand decisions,

43% of custodial decisions

30% of those dealt with by Youth Offending Teams.

At Feltham Young Offenders Institution, the only Young Offenders Institution in London **42% of the inmates are Black.**

It is well known that Britain is a country very fond of locking up its population. From 1992-2002 the British prison population grew by 55%. During this same period the Black and minority ethnic prison population grew by 124%. BME groups are over-represented at every stage of the criminal justice system from stop and search to custody. **(source: ICPR, Prison Population 2002).**

Black people of all ages are five time more likely to be in prison than white people!

As is usually the case, the situation is just as dire in the US. According to *The Real War on Crime:* **The Report of the National Criminal Justice Commission in the US**, blacks account for 13% of regular drug users but 35% of drug possession arrests, 55 % of drug possession convictions and 74 % of all drug possession prison sentences. A Black male defendant pays higher bail than a comparable white one, is significantly more likely to suffer incarceration before trial, is less likely than his white counterpart to negotiate a lenient plea bargain, and can expect to serve more time for the same crime. A Black defendant is also more likely to be sentenced to death than a white one who commits the same crime. The killer whose victim is white is 11 times more likely to be sentenced to death than the killer whose victim is Black.

The commission reports points out that, though it is true that African Americans commit proportionately more crimes than whites, it is also true that African American crime rates have remained consistent since the middle 70s. In other words Blacks are committing about the same proportion of crime as they have done for the last 40 years, but are being incarcerated more. Indeed after reviewing statistics from the U.S. Department of Justice, Jerome Miller founder of the National Centre on Institutions and Alternatives in Alexandria, Virginia has concluded that by the year 2010, the majority of Black men between the ages of 10-39 will be in jail.

(Becoming Dad – Black Men and the Journey to Fatherhood **Pitts 1999)**

Street Gangs

One of the earliest points where a young man may become involved in organised crime and violence is in a teenage gang. Gangs have been variously defined as a playgroup formed out of unconscious pressures and instinctual need (Puffer 1912), to a group derived from conflict with others (Thrasher 1927/1963), to a definitional emphasis on territoriality and delinquent behaviour (Gardner 1983). Thinking about why gangs form aids attempts at clarification. Thrasher pointed to inadequacies in family functioning, schools, housing, sanitation, employment and other community characteristics combined to help motivate youths to turn elsewhere – to a gang – for life satisfactions and rewards.

Tannenbaum (1939) proposed that the gang forms not because of its attractiveness per se, but because 'positive socio-cultural forces' – family, school, church – that might train a youth into a more socially acceptable behaviours are weak or unavailable.

In 1974, Miller conducted a major national survey seeking information related to gangs. Particular attention was paid to the six American cities reporting the highest levels of gang activity. His results confirmed that gang violence like most violence is a young male problem. Gang members in the surveyed cities were predominately male; aged 12-21; residing in the poorer, usually central city areas; and came from families at the lower occupational and educational levels. Only 5 per cent or less of gang crime is committed by females. Females join gangs later than do males and leave earlier.

There is a common misconception peddled by the media that the gang situation and gun and knife crime are problems of the Black community. The only time that mainstream (read 'white') society encounters these problems is when they spill out from the Black ghettos and innocent white by-standers (like Ben Kinsella in London or Rhys Jones in Liverpool) get caught in the crossfire. The truth is that gangs members are drawn from a locality's populous and so will be ethnically representative of that area. Glasgow has a major gang and knife crime problem, and has had for years. According to the Strathclyde Police Glasgow has a least 100 gangs, and in the region of Easterhouse there are 14 gangs in six square miles. Gang members in Glasgow and Liverpool are predominantly White, whereas gang members in Manchester and London are predominantly Black. In London the Black population increases with the level of deprivation, so it is not surprising that the racial make-up in the city's poorest areas are predominately Black. The sad truth is that 80% of Black African and Black Caribbean communities live in Neighbourhood

143

Renewal Areas which are identified as England's most deprived areas.

The higher proportion of Black gang members overall reflects the disproportionate presence of Black communities in deprived inner city neighbourhoods.

Why do males join? Largely to obtain what all adolescents seek: peer friendship, pride, identity development, enhancement of self esteem, excitement, and the acquisition of resources – goals which are often not available through legitimate means in the disorganised and low income environments from which most gang youths originate.

In their 2005 book *Freakonomics* American authors Levitt & Dubner apply economic theory to everyday popular phenomena. In one of the more interesting chapters they examine the inner workings of a drug selling gang in Chicago, and ask if drug dealers really make as much money as the popular media would have us believe, why is it that so many still live with their mothers? They also ask why, if crack dealing is the most dangerous job in America, and the salary for most of the gang members so poor, why would anyone join? Their answer nicely illuminates the problem of poverty of aspiration for those living in low budget environments.

"To kids growing up in a housing project on Chicago's south side, crack dealing seemed like a glamour profession. For many of them, the job of gang boss – highly visible and highly lucrative – was easily the best job they thought they had access to. Had they grown up under different circumstances, they might have thought about becoming economists or writers. But in the neighbourhood where J.T.'s gang operated, the path to a decent legitimate job was practically invisible. Fifty-six percent of the neighbourhood's children lived below the poverty line. 78% came from single parent homes. Fewer than 5% of the neighbourhood's adults had a college degree; barely one in three adult men worked at all.

The gang presented an opportunity for longtime employment. Before crack it was just about impossible to earn a living in a street gang. When it was time for a gangster to support a family he would have to quit…. But with crack, there was real money to be made. This was happening just as old-fashioned sort of lifetime jobs – factory jobs especially - were disappearing. With that option narrowing, crack dealing looked even better."
Levitt & Dubner (2005)

Although some of the more violent gangs in Britain do sell drugs, many do not. Most young boys do not join gangs because of a thirst for money and power, or as a

145

means to visit violence upon others. For many of their members gangs just present an opportunity for self protection and something to belong to. Or as US rapper **Snoop Dogg** said in a 2011 newspaper interview "What people don't understand is joining a gang ain't bad, it's cool, it's fine. When you in the hood, joining a gang is cool because all your friends are in the gang, all your family's in the gang. We're not just killing people every night, we're just hanging out, having a good time and we're in the gang...So it's more like a family than anything."

Never-the-less, with gang membership often comes violence, even when there is no financial gain to be had. The excellent 1991 movie *'Boyz N Tha Hood'* starring that other West Coast rapper **Ice Cube** brilliantly shows how, by just living in a certain area of Los Angeles, a young man can be drawn into the gang violence even if he doesn't want to be.

According to the report **Dying To Belong: An In-depth Review of Street Gangs in Britain** from the Centre for Social Justice, at least half of the 27 murders of young people perpetrated by young people in London in 2007 were gang related.

Strong territorial rivalries among youth affiliations can lead them to commit violent crime in order to exercise control over their area. When Superintendent Leroy Logan gave evidence to the House of Commons Home Affairs Committee in 2007 he warned of an

146

increase in postcode violence driven by 'paranoid misguided loyalties' of young people who feel threatened by the presence of strangers in their area. Staff at Feltham Young Offender Institution reported that loyalties connected to certain roads in London continued and spilt over into the prison, with incidents outside causing violence within the prison. According to one of the participants in Lambeth's gang exit programme, levels of violence have become so bad that 'you cannot even go to certain estates without being in a certain crew.. either you are with them or against them. That is the way they look at it."

What is also overstated in the media is the degree of organisation and structure in these gangs. In many cases they do not have a strict hierarchy or chain of command but are rather just a disorganised group of kids trying to make a name for themselves. As Detective Superintendent Dave Kelly said of the gang problem in Liverpool *"we are not talking about the mafia here, we are talking about kids, teenagers, who lived on a housing estate. I do not want to overstate the sophistication of these groups. In essence they are very often a collection of dysfunctional and feckless youngsters who associate purely on the geographical basis of where they live."* (quoted in The Independent 17 December 2008)

147

Dying for Respect

James Gilligan is a psychiatrist at Harvard Medical School where he directs the Center for the Study of Violence. In his books *Violence* and *Preventing Violence* he argues that acts of violence are 'attempts to ward off or eliminate the feeling of shame and humiliation and replace it with its opposite, the feeling of pride.' Gilligan goes as far as to say that he has 'yet to see a serious act of violence that was not provoked by the experience of feeling shamed and humiliated.. and that did not represent the attempt to undo this loss of face.

Inter-male violence is more likely to occur amongst those who are outside the mainstream institutions of paid employment and marriage. Homicide figures for Detroit in the 1970s indicated that unemployed men were over represented by about four times amongst both offenders and their victims. Unmarried men are also over-represented by about 60 percent. **Farrington, Berkowitz and West (1982)** found that working-class boys who reported most fights were likely to be from poorer backgrounds, and to have unstable employment records.

Wolfgang (1959) analysed the files of the Philadelphia Police Department during the period 1948-52. He found that the most frequent category was 'an altercation of relatively trivial origin; insult, curse; jostling etc. Evolutionary psychologists Martin **Daly and** Margo **Wilson** in their 1988 book *Homicide* point out that in the context these altercations become about reputation and social identity, and these are of much greater importance in male groups where the impact of the law or moral restraint are weak or absent. According to Daly and Wilson's analysis such altercations are not really about trivial matters at all, but about the relative status of the protagonists: one of them cannot back down without rendering himself subordinate in the social group. For a member of a marginal group, challenged in the presence of acquaintances he sees every day, performance in such an exchange will be crucially important for reputation, and hence self-esteem. Young men have strong incentives to achieve and maintain as high a social status as they can – because their success in sexual competition depends on status. While looks and physical attractiveness are most important for women, it is status that matter most for sexual success among men. **Campbell (1986)** noted that marginal males will have fewer alternative ways of establishing self-esteem; they are likely to be unemployed, excluded from their households for much of the time, and generally to have little access to recognised sources of status. Reputation gained in conflicts therefore becomes of crucial importance.

An important feature of masculinity is that it is achieved rather than an ascribed status. It arises from behaving in a particular way. A boy's self-esteem is derived from taking part in a range of physical activities, and there is an emphasis on toughness for defining status. During adulthood, self-esteem is derived from a wider range of activities, notably occupational achievement. As we have seen for men in marginal urban communities this source of status is generally not available. Status arises from challenges and counter challenges within the male street community.

In *Outliers* Malcolm **Gladwell** discusses the 'culture of honour'. In his examples he discusses blood feuds in the southern states of America in the 19th century, but his observations are just as applicable to the streets of any city in the 21st century.

"He has to be aggressive: he has to make it clear, through his words and deeds, that he is not weak. He has to be willing to fight in response to even the slightest challenge to his reputation – and that's what a culture of honour means. It's a world where a man's reputation is at the centre of his livelihood and self worth."
(Gladwell 2008 p 167)

In their 2009 book *The Spirit Level* authors Richard **Wilkinson** and Kate **Pickett** argue that a whole host of social problems from obesity to mental illness to teenage pregnancy are made worse by greater inequality between the rich and the poor, and violent crime is no exception.

".. the more we feel devalued by those above us and the fewer resources we have to fall back on, the greater will be the desire to regain some sense of self-worth by asserting superiority over any more vulnerable groups."

(Wilkinson & Pickett (2009) P207)

Was it Gladwell's culture of honour or the frustration of being at the bottom of the heap that led to the senseless murder of 16 year old **Ben Kinsella** in 2008? Ben was fatally stabbed after a night out with friends at a bar in Islington, north London, to celebrate the end of their GCSE exams in June of that year. Three Black youths, Juress Kika, 19, Jade Braithwaite, 18, and Michael Alleyne, 20 at the time of trial, were convicted of the murder at the Old Bailey. A row broke out and Ben was chased along the street with other youngsters - then stabbed to death when he stopped running. He was stabbed 11 times in five seconds by the three youths in revenge for the "disrespect" shown to Braithwaite earlier. At the time of the story the three youths were described by Ben's distraught parents as 'animals'.   2008 saw a media frenzy about knife crime, and each week saw a new tragic story about young lives being wasted in this way. With each new story there were more calls for tougher sentences for those caught carrying a knife, but the thought that kept occurring to me was 'what has gone wrong that would cause a teenager to stab to death another teenager who he hardly even knows?' The Detective chief inspector who led the murder inquiry offered an answer.

D.C.I John Macdonald said at the time of the trial *"Young people are obsessed about disrespect. It's becoming a massive problem. They feel that they have to respond." "Lack of parental care is a factor. The fathers disappeared, the mothers not home. There is no controlling influence. They have no social abilities whatsoever to interact with people."*

Superintendent John Sutherland of Islington borough who was interviewed at the time also believes that the breakdown of the family unit exerts a profoundly negative impact on young men.

"The number we come across from broken homes and homes where domestic violence occurs or is witnessed is frightening. They are two of the most alarming and recurring features for me."

Whereas historically gang violence would have been more directly linked to drug turf and the enforcement of debts, now violence is commonly triggered in one of two ways.

1) A single, often minor act of disrespect: for example someone looking at a gang member in the wrong way. To maintain his reputation the gang member must respond, normally through violence.

2) Territorial conflict: for example someone from a rival postcode entering a gang's territory. This is seen as an affront to the gang's power and reputation, and hence to reinforce this, the trespasser must be punished.

The causes of Crime and the government's ineptitude

"We can punish young offenders all we like, but if we don't tackle the causes of crime we'll never have a safer society"
David Cameron 2006

When **Tony Blair** famously promised that the Labour government would 'be tough on crime, and tough on the causes of crime' what was he thinking? Did he even know what the causes of crime were? He can't have acknowledged its origins in **broken families** because the Labour government did nothing to encourage families to stay together, infact the benefits system incentivised couples to separate. He can't have known that its roots were in **school exclusions** because the school league tables that the labour government promoted only encouraged schools to permanently exclude any child who wasn't going to contribute to their exam success. Did he know that the roots lie in **social inequality** because social inequality actually increased under his Labour government. No the government's approach was all wrong – it was more like 'tough on crime and tough on the _symptoms_ of crime'. In response to the rise in knife crime their solution was to increase the penalty for possession. But when a boy takes a knife from his mum's kitchen draw before leaving home, what do you think he is more worried about – the sentence if caught carrying one, or the chances of being cornered by the gang who threatened to 'wet him up' when they next saw him? For example, imagine if Damiola Taylor had survived his attack with a broken bottle. If he recovered and returned back to school, who could blame him if he then chose to carry a knife for protection? The percentage of school children reporting having carried a knife increased by more than 50% between 2002 and 2005, but as a 2008 Home Office report admitted, carrying one appears largely to be motivated by fear and not a desire to defend territory or reputation. 85% of young people who report carrying a knife claim to have done so for protection and just 4% have used it to threaten someone, and 1% to injure someone. **(Home Office, July 2008)**. When the latest horrific crime story hits the news pages the government's one dimensional response seems confined to debating the appropriate length of sentence for being caught in possession of the weapon in question. The problem is not in the weapon, it is in the mind of the young man holding the weapon. No thought seems to be given as to why a young man would feel the need to carry a knife, or join a gang. No-one seems to be addressing the root of how a young man could become so de-sensitised to violence that they would callously murder another human being in cold blood – or if they do address it they blame video games and rap lyrics! This was addressed in 2007by Professor Sir Aynsley-Green who was at that time the Children's Tsar.

"The demonization and lack of empathy for young people is a major issue for England. It causes anger and alienation. At the moment we have a youth system dominated by a punitive approach. It doesn't focus on children's needs."

I'm no fan of the Conservative party either, but one of their former leaders and Work and Pensions secretary Iain Duncan Smith through his **Centre for Social Justice** at least tried to examine the root causes of many social problems from a more holistic approach and offered solutions with a more long term perspective, rather than the quick-fix knee-jerk reaction so favoured by governments. As they observed in their report 2007 *Being Tough on the Causes of Crime: Tackling family breakdown to prevent youth crime'*

"....increasing penalties for offenders will do little to stop the next generation of prisoners and unlock the cycle of deprivation which so many young people are trapped in, unless it is accompanied by attempt to tackle the underlying drivers of crime. Yet this Government has got the balance wrong: all its energies are directed at punishing those whose lives are products of a fractured society without tackling the causes of crime in a holistic way." P4

According to the report **'the majority of young offenders come from broken homes, nearly two thirds have drug and alcohol problems, more than three in four have no educational qualifications and many young prisoners have mental health problems.**

To aid any future governments, let's really examine in detail 'the causes of crime'.

1 Broken/ Dysfunctional Families – 'Father Hunger'.

We all know children who were raised well by lone parents, but the evidence of a series of UK longitudinal studies shows strong correlations between broken homes and delinquency. 70% of young offenders come from lone-parent families. According to Levitt & Dubner in *Freakonomics*, **childhood poverty and a single parent household are the two biggest predictors that a child will have a criminal future.** As outlined in Chapter 1, Black children overall are more likely to grow up in single parent households and in most cases the heads of these households are lone mothers, but the negative effect of the absent father is more than just economic. Boys and young men who lack father involvement can develop 'father hunger', a trauma which leaves them vulnerable to peer pressure and external influences. Gangs are most commonly found in areas with a high proportion of lone parent families. The gang for a significant number of young people growing up in our most deprived communities, has become a substitute family with the gang leader as the 'father'. The lack of positive male role models has meant that the masculinity being modelled to gang involved young men is that of a hyper-alpha male. And this 'father hunger' leading to a life of crime is not just a process suffered by Black boys. In his 2000 book '*Beyond Anger – A Guide for Men*, clinical psychologist Thomas J. Harbin examines the roots of the debilitating rage and low self esteem that many men carry around with them.

"When many angry men were boys, they didn't have men around to watch as they experienced sadness, grief, joy, excitement, or tenderness. Many never had the opportunity to see how men react to physical injury, praise, the birth of a child, or the death of a loved one. Many had no fathers in the home and no reliable men to fill in for the absentee fathers."

In Harbin's mind there is no doubt that this lack of positive male role model results in boys growing up unable to cope with life's challenges.

"In my work with accused felons, I have found that probably three out of four had no men in the home when they were growing up." (Harbin, 2000)

This 'father hunger' is not just suffered by boys from impoverished backgrounds. If movie star Michael Douglas is to be believed it can also be suffered by the offspring of the super rich Hollywood elite. In 2010 Douglas' son Cameron was convicted of drug dealing in New York. Michael wrote to the judge begging for leniency, explaining that some of the blame lay with himself, as Cameron fell in with the wrong company after feeling neglected by his own father.

*(**Fractured Families** **the interim Report of the Family Breakdown Working Group**)* found that children of neglectful parents are more likely to suffer impaired psychological development and be at increased risk of drug and alcohol abuse and delinquency. Many propose that a 'propensity to

violence develops primarily from wrong treatment before the age of 3." One of the key inhibitors of developing a propensity to violence is acquiring empathy. Parental separation and family dysfunction disrupt potential and established attachment patterns preventing the acquisition of empathy.

2 Poverty

London borough profiles demonstrate that the Black population increases with the level of deprivation, as does the level of crime. It is clear that ethnicity, deprivation, victimisation and offending are closely and intricately inter-related. Part of the reason Black men are disproportionately involved in crime is that they are disproportionately concentrated into areas of poverty. **80% of Black African and Black Caribbean communities live in Neighbourhood Renewal Fund areas, those identified as England's most deprived areas.** (Tinsley & Jacobs)

The association between socio-economic disadvantage and involvement in crime among people of all ethnic groups is well established.

In the 1940s, sociologists of the Chicago school described how some neighbourhoods had persistent reputations for violence over the years – different populations moved in and out but the same poor neighbourhoods remained dangerous whoever was living in them. Such high crime neighbourhoods are typically poor areas where people can't trust one another, where there are high levels of fear and neighbours won't intervene for the common good.

More recent research in the UK has indicated that homicide rates are associated with poverty. A study of street crime conducted for the Youth Justice Board (FitzGerald, Stockdale and Hale 2003) found the main reason for young Black people's overrepresentation for street crime in London boroughs was the general level of deprivation and the proportion of households with dependent children but no earning adult. Another important factor was population turnover, implying a greater degree of anonymity for offenders and a reduced likelihood that residents would intervene to prevent or report crimes which did not directly affect them.

3 Social exclusion

Recent surveys have demonstrated the direct link between school exclusions and involvement in the criminal justice system. In their 2004 youth survey, MORI found that 60% of young people excluded from school had offended, compared to 26% of young people in mainstream education. A Home Office study found that permanent exclusion adds impetus to youth offending, setting in train sequences of events that can culminate in the onset or escalation of offending.(Berridge, et al. 2001)

Work not only provides regular income, but also provides a sense of purpose, identity and belonging. It is no coincidence that the highest prevalence of gangs is found in areas with the highest levels of general worklessness and youth unemployment: the gang is an alternative to mainstream employment, offering the same advantages.

Furthermore, young people with poor if any qualifications are unlikely to gain meaningful employment, and so activities such as drug dealing may appear an attractive alternative. It has been estimated that an Elder's (gang leader) income from street level drug dealing can be in the region of £130,000 per annum and a lowly foot soldier is around £26,000. (**Pitts, *Reluctant Gangsters***). Apart from being a professional footballer, how could a young Black man who leaves school with no qualifications ever expect to earn such a salary? Infact a university graduate will be lucky to land a first job that pays £26k.

Solutions to Problem 4 - CRIME

Those who are reading these chapters in order will have noticed how one social problem leads into the next. Thus a lot of the suggested solutions in this chapter will already have been touched on in previous chapters.

1 Find a mentor

If we accept that broken families and the syndrome of 'Father Hunger' is one of the drivers of youth crime and gang membership then we should obviously increase our efforts to sustain the Black family. As I pleaded to mothers in chapter 1, if your relationship with the child's father breaks down, don't let his relationship with his child breakdown as well. If the father is unavailable or unwilling to be involved in his son's life, then acknowledge that no matter how good a mother you are, when he reaches his teens your son will crave a father figure. Be prepared for this by putting some suitable mentors in place. It doesn't have to be someone super successful or rich and famous. In fact, real men who he can see and talk to in everyday life are more valuable than celebrities. Slightly older men who he can look up to and that you know will instil the correct values. If you don't provide them, your son will find some for himself who may not be so suitable.

162

2 Stay in School

If we know that school exclusion, leads to social exclusion and crime, then make sure that your son doesn't get excluded. And that doesn't mean going down to the school and 'kicking up a stink' when your son comes home with the letter. That means being fully involved with his education from day one – not trying to fight the fire when it's already blazing!

3 Move!!

Even if you are providing a stable family environment complete with two loving parents and instilling the correct values, and even if your son has his 'head on straight' and is working hard at school, if you're a living in the wrong area the gangs and crime will find him. Remember Damiola Taylor was a good, hard-working boy on his way home from his after-school computer club when he was stabbed. On some of these estates, young boys either become members of gangs or victims of them, and there is nothing you can do to prevent it other than to get him out of that toxic environment.

References for Chapter 4

Berridge, D. Brodie, I., Pitts, J., Porteous, D., & Tarling, R., (2001) – *The Independent effects of permanent exclusion from school on the offending careers of young people.* Home Office

Biddulph, S. (1998) *Raising Boys.* London. Thorsons

The Centre for Social Justice (2007) '*Being Tough on the Causes of Crime: Tackling family breakdown to prevent youth crime*'

The Centre for Social Justice (2009) *Dying To Belong: An In-depth Review of Street Gangs in Britain*

Campbell, A (1986) 'The Streets and Violence' in A. Campbell and J.J. Gibbs (eds), *Violent Transactions: The Limits of Personality*, Oxford: Blackwell, pp 115-32.

Daly, M & Wilson, M (1988) *Homicide*, New York: Aldine de Gruyter.

Daly, M & Wilson, M (1990) '*Killing The Competition : female/female and male/male competition*', Human Nature 1: 81-107

Dubner, S.J and Levitt, S.D.. (2005). *Freakonomics – A Rogue Economist Explores the Hidden Side of Everything.* London. Penguin

Farrington, D.P., Berkowitz, L and West D.J. (1982) 'Differences between individual and group fights', *British Journal of Social Psychology*, 21: 323-33

Fitzgerald, Stockdale and Hale (2003) *Young People and Street Crime.* London Youth Justice Board

Gilligan, J. (2001) *Preventing Violence.* New York. Thames & Hudson

Gilligan, J. (1996) *Violence: Our Deadly Epidemic and its Causes.* New York. G.P. Putnam

Gladwell, M. (2008) *Outliers – The Story of Success.* Penguin Books (London)
Harbin T. J. (2000) '*Beyond Anger – A Guide for Men'.* New York. Malowe & Company

House of Commons Home Affairs Committee (2007) *Young Black People and the Criminal Justice System*

McLagan, G. (2005) *Guns & Gangs.* Allison & Busby

Pickett, K. Wilkinson, R. (2009) *The Spirit Level – Why Equality is Better for Everyone.*   London (Penguin Books Ltd.

Pitts, J. (2007) *Reluctant Gangsters: Youth Gangs In Waltham Forest.* University of Bedfordshire

Pitts, L. (1999) *Becoming Dad – Black Men and the Journey to Fatherhood.* Canada. Agate Books.

Puffer J.A. (1912) *The Boy and His Gang*, Boston: Houghton Mifflin.

Roe, S. Ashe, A. *Young People and Crime: findings from the 2006 Offending, Crime and Justice Survey,* Home Office Statistical Bulletin (Home Office, July 2008)

Tannenbaum (1939) *Crime and Community*, New York: Columbia University Press

Thrasher F.M. 1927/1963) *The Gang*, Chicago: University of Chicago Press.

Tinsley, J. Jacobs, M. (2006) *Deprivation and Ethnicity in England – A Regional Perspective* Regional Trends 39.

Wolfang, M. E. (1958) *Patterns of Criminal Homicide*, Philadelphia, PA: University Pennsylvania Press.

PROBLEM 5
Mental Health
Is Britain driving us mad?

"Have you forgotten that when we were brought here,
we were robbed of our name,
Robbed of our language,
We lost our religion, our culture, our God?
And many of us by the way we act,
We even lost our minds!"
Dr Khallid Muhammed
sampled by Public Enemy on *Night of the*
Living Baseheads.

Introduction - Colourful eccentrics, Government Conspiracies & Paranoia.

When I used to work in south London in the mid '90s, on leaving Brixton tube station I was often greeted by a brother who could be most kindly described as 'colourful'. With a red, gold and green hat perched atop of his head of dreadlocks, he was always on a bicycle which he had customised with various ribbons, mirrors and red, gold and green tape wrapped around all of the tubing. Perched on the handlebars was what we used to call a 'ghetto blaster', the speakers of which were also painted red, gold and green and the body of which was covered in various messages hand scrawled in white paint. He would regularly lecture the crowd on the evils of Queen Elizabeth and 'Babylon system'. Such figures are regular features in many Black communities and are usually dismissed as harmless eccentrics. This eccentricity can even be encouraged if it is accompanied by some kind of musical talent as is the case with musicians like Lee 'Scratch' Perry in Jamaica, or George Clinton and Sun Ra in the States, all of whom claimed to be visitors from another planet or at least in possession of a higher knowledge.

Views of the world which are outside of the mainstream, are a constant feature in our community.

168

Go to any Black party or family gathering or listen to any Black radio phone-in show and you will often find people who subscribe to conspiracy theories such as the idea that Princess Diana was assassinated by MI5 under the orders of the Royal family; or that Martin Luther King, Malcolm X and the Kennedy Brothers were all assassinated by agents acting for the government in order to keep Blacks down; or that the Twin towers were actually destroyed with the collusion of the US government so that they could get away with a more aggressive foreign policy and more draconian measures of state control at home. Or the wildest theory, (that my grandfather used to subscribe to) that the Apollo moon landings were faked, because human beings could not in reality have survived the journey into space.

But our friend in Brixton and our Black radio show callers need to be careful when and where they air their opinions. Outside Brixton tube station our friend was dismissed by the commuters as a harmless 'nutter', but in a different place and a different context he could have found himself in the back of a police van, detained under section 136 of the Mental Health Act.

But are such theories so irrational? It is a fact that two of Black American's most charismatic leaders were both felled by assassin's bullets, and of the three American Presidents to have been assassinated, one freed the slaves (Abraham Lincoln) and the other was a supporter of civil rights legislation. Is it any wonder then that many Black people feel that the government is actively involved in an on-going campaign to keep them down? Back in 2008 I was one of many Black people who argued that Barack Obama would never become President because he would be assassinated first.

Sadly for many from the Black community, these unorthodox views and conspiracy theories become something more than just an interesting topic for debate at a party, but rather something that prevents normal functioning in society. Something that becomes so debilitating and dangerous, that they have to be forcibly removed from the community. One such case involved **Peter Bryan.**

Bryan, who suffers from schizophrenia, was originally convicted of manslaughter in 1994 after he beat a 20 year old shop assistant to death. A judge ruled that he should be detained indefinitely at a high security hospital, but by 2002 a Mental Health Review Tribunal gave permission for his release to a hostel in North London under supervision by psychiatrists.

At the beginning of 2004 Bryan was transferred to low support accommodation. In February he was given permission to leave the ward temporarily, but he went straight to a DIY shop where he bought a claw

170

hammer, a Stanley knife and a screwdriver and went to visit old friend Brian Cherry. When the Police, who were alerted by the neighbours, arrived at Mr Cherry's flat, they found Peter Bryan covered in blood having battered Mr Cherry to death with the hammer, sawed off both his arms and left leg, scooped his brains from his skull and fried them in butter before eating them. After the killing Bryan was sent to Broadmoor High Security hospital but came to public attention again when he assaulted another inmate who later died of his injuries.

This is one of the more disturbing high profile cases featuring a Black men suffering with mental illness, but up and down the country there are Black men and women who have spent the majority of their adult lives in an out of Psychiatric units, their mood and behaviour regulated by medication. The case of Peter Bryan was obviously an extreme case – only a tiny minority of people suffering mental illness ever harm other people. They are in fact much more likely to harm themselves. But when Black people do experience a decline in their mental wellbeing they may be far more unlikely to seek professional help, for mental health services are seen, like the judiciary, as just another arm of the repressive state. The case of **Roger Sylvester** helps to reinforce this view.

On January 11, 1999, police arrived outside Sylvester's house as a result of a 999 emergency call. Two officers came to the house initially and found him naked in his front garden. Within minutes another six officers had arrived. The eight officers put Sylvester to the ground where he was handcuffed. He was detained under Section 136 of the Mental Health Act. Police officers told his family that he was restrained "for his own safety." But they admitted that he had not been violent or aggressive towards the police or anybody else. According to one witness, Sylvester's body was already limp when it was placed in the police van. He was taken to St Ann's hospital and carried from the van to a private room where, still restrained, he was put on the floor by upwards of six police officers for nearly 20 minutes before being seen by a doctor. While the doctor left the room to get some medication, Sylvester went limp and collapsed. The officers, with the assistance of medical staff, tried to resuscitate him but he had sustained numerous injuries and remained in a coma at the Whittington hospital until his life support machine was switched off seven days later.

Britain's Black Community and Mental Illness – the stats

It is quite appropriate that the chapter on mental illness should follow on from the chapter on Crime, as for Black people the criminal justice system often acts as a gateway to the mental health system. Recent figures show that **Black communities are over 40% more likely than average to be referred to mental health services through the criminal justice system.** The Fourth National Survey of Ethnic Minorities (FNS) shows a higher rate of psychotic illness for Black Caribbean people than for white people, with **Black Caribbean people being twice as likely as white people to be diagnosed with psychosis.**

A substantial body of research shows that this group is disproportionately represented in mental health statistics. For example, the Commission for Healthcare Audit and Inspection's (2007) report on a one day census of mental health inpatient wards in England found that for African and Caribbean people: the rates of admission to hospital were three times higher than average; referral rates from general practitioners were lower than average; and rates of referral from the criminal justice system were higher than average; there was greater involvement of police in referrals; rates of detention under the Mental Health Act 1983 were between 19 and 38 per cent higher than average; there were higher rates of detention in medium and high secure wards; and there were higher rates of control and restraint.

A training pack from the University of Manchester's Department of Health (1996) identifies similar issues in relation to the care and treatment of Black people with mental health problems:

Firstly, the disproportionate numbers of African-Caribbeans in psychiatric wards, particularly the higher rates for compulsory detention under the Mental Health Act 1983, for people of African Caribbean origin, and also for some people of Asian origins.

Second, there have been reports of more compulsory admissions of Black patients under the 'forensic' sections of the Mental Health Act, and more transfers of patients to secure wards for reasons unconnected with violence.

Third, one study found that people from the Caribbean living in stable families were more likely to be admitted to hospital by the police, rather than through GP's.

There is also evidence that African-Caribbean people with mental health problems are more likely to receive medication as the primary form of treatment , are less likely to receive psychotherapy, and are increasingly likely to attempt suicide (McKenzie et al 2001).

Higher than expected rates of schizophrenia among African-Caribbeans living in England were reported as early as the 1960s, (Kiev 1965), and consistently thereafter. In the late 1980s several studies reported the rates were even higher in the British born children of the immigrants (McGovern & Cope, 1987; Harrison et al 1988).

There is a clear consensus that minority groups are represented within psychiatric settings in a different way, both quantitatively and qualitatively, from the white majority. There are two ways of addressing this apparent discrepancy. The first is based on the notion of disease variability, that ethnic minority groups have higher rates of mental illness compared to white people, and that psychiatric services show a different pattern of service usage as a result. The second explanation is based on the view that such variation in services are fundamentally to do with how European psychiatry discriminates against Black people. I shall address both of these perspectives.

Differential treatment by services

A study of compulsorily detained patients at the Maudsley Hospital (Moodley and Thornicroft, 1988) showed that all the West Indian patients were detained in a locked ward at the time of admission, compared with half of the White men, and that medication was more likely to be administered immediately to Black men than to White detained patients. In a study in Nottingham (Chen et al, 1991) a depot injection was more likely to be given to African Caribbeans than to

175

other ethnic groups and it was also given earlier in the course of treatment. Seclusion was used more commonly for Black patients (compared to whites) at a US university hospital (Soloff and Turner, 1981), explained by researchers as resulting from attribution (to Black patients) of violent traits, cultural prejudice, fear and distrust…compromising the quality of understanding between patient and staff and contributing ultimately to a system of bias in seclusion practice. Figures for 2005 show that Black patients were still more likely to experience physical seclusion and restraint than other groups, with figures for 2006 revealing a particularly high rate of hands-on restraint for this group.

Examining Schizophrenia

The DSM is the guidebook for mental health practitioners detailing definitions, symptoms and suitable treatments for all mental illnesses. According to DSM III-R, (American Psychiatric Association 1980) schizophrenia represents a group of disorders characterised by the presence of thought disorder. The DSM directs attention to the patients' misinterpretations of reality; delusions and hallucinations; inappropriate emotional and social response; and withdrawn regressive, or bizarre behaviour.

Although delusions vary, they tend to encompass a small number of themes. The most common type is persecutory or paranoid in which the individual feels himself the victim of some kind of malevolent plot. The imaginary persecutors are sometimes people known to the patient, but more often institutions such as government bodies or criminal gangs or ideological groups.

Grandiose delusions embrace four main themes: beliefs that the individual has some type of special powers, is wealthy, has some kind of special mission, or has some type of special identity. Often they occur with persecutory delusions or delusions of reference, in which innocuous events are held to have some special significance.

It is possible that delusional beliefs, even if clearly unrealistic, contain a nugget of truth that is distorted by the delusional process. Mirowsky and Ross studied persecutory beliefs in a survey of 500 randomly selected residents of El Paso, Texas. Mirowsky and Ross were able to show that in their sample, persecutory beliefs, beliefs about external control and mistrusts were connected to socio-economic status and educational attainment.

So why would Black people be particular prone to suffering from this disease? Like the debate in education that splits into the two camps arguing for external causes or internal causes, the mental health

177

debate enjoys a similar dichotomy between those factors that come from within us, and those that come from the hostile external environment. Lets examine all the theories more closely.

a) Genetic predisposition

This used to be the favourite explanation of mental health professionals. Since schizophrenia is generally thought to be under considerable genetic influence, genetic predisposition among the African-Caribbean population has been investigated. Both Sugarman & Craufurd (1994) and Hutchinson et al (1996) found that the risk of developing schizophrenia was similar for parents and siblings of both White patients and first generation African-Caribbean patients. However the siblings of second generation schizophrenia patients had a risk for schizophrenia that was markedly higher than their white counterparts suggesting that strong environmental factors are acting on the second generation African-Caribbeans, and that individuals from certain families may be particularly vulnerable (Hutchinson et al 1996.)

89 percent of all schizophrenics do not have a schizophrenic parent and 81 percent do not have a schizophrenic parent, sister or brother. Nevertheless, years of research confirm that schizophrenia, or a tendency towards developing it, is strongly influenced

178

by familial factors, both genetic and environmental. From its earliest descriptions, schizophrenia was said to run in families. That tendency could implicate either genes or environment, or a combination of both. It is known that something goes wrong chemically and/or physically in the brain of the schizophrenic, but it is not known yet what. The antipsychotic drugs used to treat schizophrenia give clues about excesses or deficiencies of various neurotransmitter substances or receptor sites in the brain, but these are only clues. We know that about 87 percent of persons with a schizophrenic parent do not develop clinically overt cases of schizophrenia. But what about when both parents are schizophrenic?

Despite the rarity of such matings there are five completed studies to learn from. In these studies cited in Gottesman (1991) about one third of the children of two schizophrenic parents were schizophrenic. These results seem to smash the arguments for genetic inheritance.

"If schizophrenia were caused by a dominant gene, 75 percent of the children would be affected. If it were a recessive, 100 percent would be. If it were transmitted simply by exposure to schizophrenic parents or parenting, 100 percent would be. With appropriate correction for age, this yields a lifetime maximum risk of 46 percent." Gottesman (1991) p 101.

So if schizophrenia was solely down to genetic factors then the offspring of two parents with the disease would inevitable get it, but this is not the case. Therefore some other factors must be at work

b) Racism in medical profession/ misdiagnosis

Western categories of illness and their imposition in other cultures during the diagnostic process has been seriously questioned by many people, the best known being Arthur Kleinman (1977), who has proposed the term 'category fallacy' for the well known error of imposing constructions (of illness) derived in one culture in a very different cultural context. Fernando is also a strong advocate of the overrepresentation of Black patients on psychiatric wards being down to the unwitting racism of psychiatrists.

"Clinical judgement is the expertise of psychiatry, the basic training that psychiatrists get is to exercise clinical judgement but such judgement is not evidence based, but based on intuition and experience; ...the extent to which culturally induced distortions and racist ideologies determine the result of clinical judgment is immense." Fernando et al 1998

Simon et al, (1973) demonstrated that routine hospital diagnosis yielded a higher rate of schizophrenia and a lower rate of depression among Black patients, but these differences vanished when a structured mental state examination was used. Adebimpe (1994) has

180

pointed out that in prospective studies the observers' preconceived ideas of the rates of illness in two racial groups in a study may contaminate their recognition of symptom patterns and the process of making a diagnosis. It can be argued that the training that precedes the application of structured interviews and diagnostic rating instruments builds in a bias in researchers. In an environment where professional folklore emphasises an epidemic of schizophrenia in black people, the thrusts of the training and subsequent research projects constitute an exercise in describing this 'epidemic'.

Mukherjee et al, (1983) reviewed the records of 76 bi-polar patients in an out-patient department of an inner city hospital. Ethnicity showed a significant association with misdiagnosis – Blacks and Hispanics having been misdiagnosed more often than whites.

Adebimpe et al, (1982) using a structured interview to review 273 patients with a diagnosis of schizophrenia, showed some symptoms appeared more severely among Black than among white patients. Black patients were deemed to be more angry, impulsive, hallucinatory, dysphoric and asocial than their white counterparts.

So clearly the preconceptions of doctors plays a significant role in the diagnostic process. But even if a large number of psychiatric patients are misdiagnosed, they still must have presented with some form of mental distress to find themselves infront of a psychiatrist in the first place.

c) Racism in society/environmental factors

Another large blow is dealt to the genetic predisposition argument by the fact that the over representation of African-Caribbeans in Britain are at odds with the incidence rates reported for Caribbean countries. The incidence of schizophrenia in Jamaica (Hicking & Rodger-Johnson, 1995), Trinidad (Bhugra et al, 1996) and Barbados (Mahy et al, 1999) has been found to be similar to the rate for the white population in England.

The research literature contains several hints that long-term exposure to a stressful social environment can contribute to the development of madness. One hint comes from the over-representation of people with paranoid or manic symptoms among immigrant populations. Obvious biological factors appear to be ruled out by finding that incidence rates of psychosis in the Caribbean are no higher than in other countries, by the observation that the children of Afro-Caribbean immigrants are especially vulnerable, and by the recent discovery that immigrant groups in other parts of the world are similarly affected – for example, Surinamese immigrants to Holland, East African immigrants to Sweden, migrants to Germany, and even Afro-Caribbeans returning to Jamaican after a

182

period of living in Britain. Further evidence that the critical factor is something to do with different ethnic groups mixing closely has emerged from a recent study carried out in London, in which the researchers analysed the incidence of psychotic illness in different neighbourhoods. It was found that non-white people living in white neighbourhoods are more likely to become psychotic than non-white people living in predominantly non-white neighbourhoods. Exposure to racial tension, it seems can really drive people mad. (Bentall, 2003)

"There is no doubt that the damage done by a worldview which has racism as an inherent part, adversely affects the mental health of Black people. The legacy of devaluation and demoralisation engendered by this racist worldview has combined to create a spiritual destitution (whether conscious or unconscious) among Black people in the Diaspora. The effects of this deliberate creation of 'separateness' and of being made to feel inferior are responsible for the disconnectedness which is at the root of much of the emotional damage which contributes to the mental ill-health of Black people." (Stephen 1996)

d) Alienation/identity crisis
Fernando (1998) argues that the causes of justified anger arising from racism in society are not often

183

recognised during psychiatric assessments because the black experience in society is not given credence, even if the existence of personal discrimination is recognised in a theoretical sort of way. The alienation felt by most black people is usually seen as their problem (and this often leads to 'treatment' aimed at getting people to recognise 'reality'), rather than a problem for society as a whole. But the psychological damage done to immigrants is about much more than just experiencing 'the slings and arrows' of daily racism. Some would argue that at the heart of the problem is the lack of a sense of belonging, not feeling at home in the host country, but neither having a sense of a foreign home to go back to.

According to Canadian psychologist **John Berry,** when people move from one culture to another, the outcome of this process can be one of four kinds depending on whether the individual chooses to identify with her culture of origin or with the host culture.

Integration occurs when the individual identifies with and exhibits some characteristics of both cultures. *Assimilation* occurs when the host culture is embraced and the culture of origin is disowned. *Separation* is the outcome when the individual retains the identity of her culture of origin and rejects the host culture. *Marginalization* occurs when the individual feels uncommitted to either culture. Though the first wave of Caribbean immigrants may have come to Britain with intention to assimilate, the hostile welcome that they received let them know in no uncertain terms that this would not be possible. Their children's generation were left to either try and integrate or separate, but the small size of the Caribbean community, and the weak hold that the second generation had on their parents culture often left them marginalised. As Bentall, (2003) argues that because the children of immigrants may be at special risk of becoming trapped between two identity groups and rejected by both, it is possible that they will be especially likely to suffer this marginalization, which according to Berry is the most stressful of the four.

Isolating the Causes

Although this chapter dealing with mental illness is the last of the book, it was the one that I wrote first. The issue of the disproportion of schizophrenia in the Black community was the topic that I chose to examine for the Research project for my Masters degree in Psychology (hence the more scientific tone of this chapter). As well as reading all the existing literature on the topic I went further and interviewed the subjects themselves, members of the Black British community who had a received psychiatric diagnosis, and asked them what factors they felt contributed to the breakdown in their mental health. The content of their interviews was then analysed and common themes brought out. It was actually this process that gave me the idea for this book, because it soon became clear to me that there was no one cause, but rather various intertwined factors – those factors I have tackled one by one, in the proceeding four chapters.

The interviews that I conducted for the Research Project were done 'one –on-one', and lasted anywhere between 15 and 75 minutes. The interview structure was loose, but areas covered by questions all looked at experiences that may have contributed to the decline in their mental health. Questions included: 'Did your parents remain together throughout your childhood?' 'How did you come into contact with mental health services?' and 'Have any other members of your family had a psychiatric diagnosis?'

As already outlined earlier in this chapter, it has been a long held view that schizophrenia is a genetically inherited disease, and it was clear from my sample that it does indeed run in families. One respondent has an older sister who has also been diagnosed with schizophrenia and has been in and out of hospital for the last 12 years. Another had a sister who, like him, was diagnosed with schizophrenia. Another has four brothers and four sisters, and out of the nine of them, four have a mental illness, and for three of them its schizophrenia.

The most frequently occurring theme, occurring in all but two of the interviews, was the traumatic effect of family breakdown. This manifested itself either as the effect on the mother of a relationship breakdown with her male partner, or the stress of single motherhood, or the effect on the child of separation from a parent. All of the female subjects were either single mothers at the time of their breakdowns or became so later. All were lacking in support from a male partner.

Psychologists have long argued that the quality of maternal care affects the development of the personality of the child. Ainsworth (1974) argued the more sensitive, responsive and co-operative the mother is towards the child in its early years, the more likely the child will develop a secure attachment in childhood, and go onto develop stable relationships in adulthood. But if a mother is attempting to raise a family on her own, and is getting neither financial or emotional support from the father, the negative feelings/stress/depression that the mother will naturally feel may not only affect her mental health but may well also affect the development and later mental health of the children. Bowlby's Maternal Deprivation Hypothesis (1953) argues that maternal deprivation has long term consequences leading to

187

emotional psychopathy and delinquency – a topic that I touched on in the chapter on crime.

There has been much written about the differential experience of African-Caribbean's within mental health services. Much of the work, particularly by authors such as Sashidharan and Fernando, has blamed the racism of clinicians for the over-representation of African-Caribbeans in psychiatric settings. Whilst I do not doubt that institutional racism exists within the health service, if we put that aside, Black people are still becoming mentally ill in greater numbers than their presence in the population would lead us to expect.

From my own research I believe that Black people become psychotic for much the same reasons as white people do. They are no more genetically predisposed to developing schizophrenia than they are to being excluded from school or to receiving a custodial sentence. Their preponderance is a social ill, not a genetically inherited medical one. The disproportionate rates are I feel, due to the disproportionate rate that Black people experience the life stressors known to tip people over into madness – those stressors that I have been outlining throughout this book.

Nazroo and King (2002) in their study 'Psychosis – symptoms and estimated rates' showed that those from a poorer background were more likely to suffer from a psychotic illness, and those living in inner cities were at higher risk. This was the case for White people as well as Black people and these findings support the theory that mental illness is related to living conditions rather than ethnicity or race.

Broken Families

African Caribbean children in London are more likely than White children to have been exposed to social factors known to be associated with childhood psychiatric disorder. African-Caribbean children with diagnoses of psychiatric disorders are especially likely to have had experiences such as coming from one-parent families, separation from parents, and being in children's homes or foster care (Maughan, 1989), events suffered by the majority of my respondents. A higher proportion in the Black community have experienced the trauma of family breakdown and single parent families.

In a study of Afro-Caribbean schizophrenia patients living in London carried out by psychiatrist Dinesh Bhugra (1997) of 38 Afro-Caribbean patients studied, 12 (34%) had suffered separation from their mothers for a period of four years of longer during childhood, and 19 (53%) had suffered a similar period of separation from their fathers.

Social isolation

Paradoxically, despite being known for having large and loving extended families, members of the Black British community suffer more social isolation than in the wider community. More people live alone (Burnet et al, 1999), more are unemployed (Bhugra et al, 1997) and more are imprisoned: any of these factors may result in a form of social exclusion.

Fear of Services means that neurosis leads to psychosis

From my time working on Psychiatric wards it was quickly apparent to me that there was a difference in the way that the Black and white patients presented themselves. Whilst quite often the Black patients were younger they were clearly very seriously ill – they were highly delusional and danger to themselves and others. Whilst some of the white patients presented similarly, there were also many older ones who just seemed to be a little down. They had a grip on reality, could hold a decent conversation but were just a bit depressed. This is the difference between psychosis and neurosis. Neurotic diseases include Obsessive Compulsive Disorders, Anxiety, and Depression. These are problems that many of us may face at some time of our lives but if dealt with early can be overcome. Psychosis on the other hand is a lot more debilitating and more difficult to treat. If you are struggling for a long time with a neurotic ailment that goes without treatment it can become more serious and turn into a psychotic illness.

Fear of mental health services (see *Breaking the Cycles of Fear*) leads to an unwillingness to engage with services and so results in non-treatment for the early signs of neurosis. On average there is a delay of 12 months between the onset of positive symptoms and first treatment, and delays in first treatment is robustly linked with poor early outcome (Norman & Malla, 2001). Large numbers of studies on first onset psychosis that show that where the duration of untreated psychosis (DUP) is very long, that long DUP is associated with poor outcome. Lobel et al (1993) suggest that there is evidence that the response to drug treatment later in the course of illness is slower and incomplete. Long delays increase the chance of use of the Mental Health Act 1983 and its use breeds service disengagement. Early use of the Mental Health Act increases the likelihood of its further use, with young Black males particularly at risk.

Even after clinical treatment and discharge, mental health outcomes of Black patients are shown to be poorer in terms of readmissions. Poorer clinical outcome has been associated with living alone, unemployment, conviction and imprisonment. (Bhui et al, 1998).

Conclusion

So we can see that at every stage of the course of mental illness (the causal factors in early life, the delay in seeking treatment due to fear of services, the use of coersion and the involvement of forensic services, the misdiagnosis and mistreatment by services, and poorer living conditions on discharge) Black patients fare worse than their white counterparts. Thus if we focus solely on the higher rates of psychosis suffered by African-Caribbeans, we are focussing only on the end of a long process. Thus we should be focussing not on why African-Caribbeans are disproportionately suffering from psychosis, but rather why they are disproportionately suffering the social and economic disadvantage that can lead to depression and mental illness. As I hope I have shown, it is this social and economic disadvantage that can bring with it a chain of events that can eventually lead to psychosis.

"Like many before me, I have come to the conclusion that it is grossly inaccurate to depict depression, anxiety, or even schizophrenia and other psychoses, as physical diseases of the body requiring medical

192

treatment. Although it is still possible that in some cases, sometimes genes may affect our vulnerability to distress, the massive differences that exist between rates in different nations and different groups within nations strongly suggest that genes play a minimal role in the vast majority of cases. Cards on the table, I contend that most emotional distress is best understood as a rational response to sick societies."
James (2007)

Solutions to Problem 5

1 Keep the Family Together part 1 – the nuclear family

Yes this old chestnut again. Since African-Caribbean children with diagnoses of psychiatric disorders are especially likely to have had experiences such as coming from one-parent families, separation from parents, and being in children's homes or foster care, if we want our children to stay well mentally these are experiences we need to help them avoid.

2 Keep the Family Together part 2 – the extended family

In adulthood, social isolation is another challenge to our mental wellbeing. If you are unemployed, and living alone, then it is easy for loneliness and depression to follow. Too often teenage boys get thrown out of home due to their own behaviour but are simply not ready to live on their own. A strong extended family of supportive grandparents, aunts, uncles and cousins can supply a safety net to catch those young men who can no longer live with their mothers. And if you do have family members who choose to live on their own, check on them regularly, letting them know that there is someone who they can call on if they need support.

3 Don't Be Afraid to seek professional help.

Many Black people have a fear of the mental health services, which is why they often arrive on psychiatric wards brought kicking and screaming in handcuffs by the Police, rather than being referred by their G.P and escorted by concerned relatives. But if they had the confidence in mental health services to seek help earlier on, their symptoms could have been tackled earlier and a stay in hospital may not even have been necessary.

4 Keep the family together part 3 – the community
Even after clinical treatment and discharge, mental health outcomes of Black patients are shown to be poorer in terms of re-admissions. Poorer clinical outcome has been associated with a lack of social support - living alone, unemployment, conviction and imprisonment – so we as a community need to give more social support. Even after our sons have been excluded/ evicted/convicted we must not continue the process of social isolation. We – the extended family – must make them feel welcome in our homes and offer them the necessary support to help re-integrate them into society, even if they have been rejected by the mainstream

References for Chapter 5

Adebimpe, V.R., Chu, C.C., Klein, H.E., (1982) Racial and geographic differences in the psychopathology of schizophrenia. *American Journal of Psychiatry,* 139, 888-891.

Adebimpe (1994) 'American Blacks and Psychology', *Transcultural Psychiatric Research Review*, 21, 83-111.

American Psychiatric Association (1980) *Diagnostic and Statistical Manual of Mental Disorders*, Third ed. APA, Washington, D.C.

Bentall, R.P., Kinderman, P. & Kaney, S. (1994) The self attributional process and abnormal beliefs: towards a model of persecutory delusions. *Behaviour Research and Therapy, 32,* 331-341.

Bentall, R.P. (2003) *Madness Explained: Psychosis and Human Nature.* London Penguin Books.

Berthoud, R. (1999) *Young Caribbean Men and the Labour Market: A comparison with other ethnic groups,* York: York Publishing Services and Joseph Rowntree Foundation.

Bhugra, D., Hilwig, M., Hossein, B (1996) First contact incidence rates of schizophrenia in Trinidad and one year follow up. *British Journal of Psychiatry, 169,* 587-592

Bhugra, D., Leff, J., Mallet, R., (1997). Incidence and outcome of schizophrenia in whites, African-Caribbean and Asians in London. *Psychological Medicine,* 27, 791-798.

Bhui, K., Brown, P., Hardie ,T., Watson, J.P and J. Parrot (1998). 'African- Caribbean men remanded to Brixton prison. Psychiatric and forensic characteristics and outcome of final court appearance.' *British Journal of Psychiatry* 172: 337-344

Burnett, R., Mallett, R., Bhugra, D., (1999). The first contact of patients with schizophrenia with psychiatric services: social factors and pathways to care in a multi-ethnic population. *Psychological Medicine, 11,* 581-599.

Chen, E. Y. H., Harrison, G. and Standon, P. (1991). Management of the first episode of psychotic illness in Afro-Caribbean patients', *British Journal of Psychiatry,* 158, 517-22

Commission for Healthcare Audit and Inspection's (2007) *Count Me In*, Results of a national census of inpatients in mental health hospitals and facilities in England and Wales.

Cox, J. L. (1977). Aspects of transcultural psychiatry. *British Journal of Psychiatry,* 130, 211-221

Fernando, S., Ndegwa, D. Wilson, M., (1998) *Forensic Psychiatry, Race and Culture.* London, Routledge.

Gelder, M., Gath, D. and Mayou, R. (1989) *Oxford Textbook of Psychiatry*, Oxford: Oxford University Press, 2nd edn.

Gottesman, I. (1991) *Schizophrenia genesis: the origins of madness.* New York. W.H. Freeman and Company.

Harrison, G., Owens, D., Holton, A.., (1988). A prospective study of severe mental disorder in Afro-Caribbean patients. *Psychological Medicine*, 18, 643-657.

Hicking,F. W. & Rodgers-Johnson, P. (1995) The incidence of first contact schizophrenia in Jamaica, *British Journal of Psychiatry*, 167, 193-196.

Hutchinson, J., Takei, N., Fahy, T. A. (1996) Morbid risk of schizophrenia in first degree relatives of white and African Caribbean patients with psychosis. *British Journal of Psychiatry,, 169, 776-780*

James, O. (2004) *They Fuck You Up – The Guide to Surviving Family Life*. London. Vermillion

James, O. (2007) *Afluenza* . London. Vermillion

Johannessen (1996) Early detection and intervention with schizophrenia. Schizophrenia Bulletin 1996

Keating, F. (2007) *African and Caribbean men and Mental health. A Race Equality Foundation Briefing Paper.* London, Race Equality Foundation.

Kiev, A. (1965) Psychiatric morbidity of West Indian immigrants in an urban group practice. *British Journal of Psychiatry,* 111, 51-56

Kinderman, P., & Bentall. R.P. (1996) Self discrepancies and persecutory delusions: evidence for model of paranoid ideation. *Journal of Abnormal Psychology,* 105, 106-113

Kleinman, A. R. (1977) 'Depression, somatization and the "New Cross-Cultural Psychiatry", *Social Science and Medicine*, 11 3-10.

Larsen TK et al (2000) Can duration of untreated illness be reduced? In *Early Intervention in Psychosis: a guide to concepts, evidence and interventions.* Birchwood M et al (eds) Chicester, Wiley Publications.

Littlewood, R. & Lipsedge, M. (1982) *Aliens and Alienists.* London: Penguin.

Macpherson of Cluny, Sir William, (1999). *The Stephen Lawrence Inquiry*, London: The Stationary Office.

McLeod, J. (2001): Qualitative research in counselling and psychotherapy. Sage

Mahy, G. E., Mallett, R., Leff, J., (1999) First – contact incidence-rate of schizophrenia in Barbados. *British Journal of Psychiatry,* 175, 28-33

Maughan, B. (1989) Growing up in the inner city. *Paediatric and Perinatal Epidemiology*, 3, 195-215.
McGovern, D & Cope, R (1987). First psychotic admission rates of first and second generation African-Caribbean, *Social Psychiatry,* 22, 139-149;

McKenzie, K., Samele, C., van Horn, E., Tatten, T., van Os, J. and Murray, R.B. (2001). 'Comparison of the outcome of the treatment of psychosis for people of Caribbean origin living in the UK and British Whites: report from the UK700 trail', *British Journal of Psychiatry,* 178, pp 160-5.

Mirowsky J.and Ross C.E. (1983) 'Paranoia and the structure of powerlessness', *American Sociological Review,* 48: 228-39

Moodley, P.and Thornicroft, G. (1988) 'Ethnic group and compulsory detention,' *Medicine, Science and the Law*, 28, 324-8

Mukherjee, S., Shukla, S., Woodle, J., Rosen, A. M. and Olarte, S. (1983). 'Misdiagnosis of schizophrenia in bi-polar patients: a multi-ethnic comparison'. *American Journal of Psychiatry,* 140, 157-2.

Nazroo, J., King M., (2002), 'Psychosis – symptoms and estimated rates' in Sproston, K., Nazroo, J., (ed) Ethnic Minority Psychiatric Illness Rates in the Community (Empiric), National Centre for Social Research, TSO.

Norman, R M.; Malla, A. K. (2001) Duration of untreated psychosis: a critical examination of the concept and its importance. Psychological Medicine. 31(3):381-400, April 2001.

Neighbors, H. W., Jackson, J. S., Broman, C et al (1996) Racism and the mental health of African-Americans: the role of self and system blame. *Ethnicity and Disease,* 6, 167-175

Parker, S. & Kleiner,R. (1966) *Mental Illness in the Urban Negro Community*. New York: Free Press.

Rendon, M.(1984) Myths and Stereotypes in minority groups', *International Journal of Social Psychiatry,* 30, 297-309.

The Sainsburys Centre for Mental Health (2002) Breaking the Circles of Fear – A review of the relationships between mental health services and the African and Caribbean Communities. The Sainsburys Centre for Mental Health (London)

Sashidharan, S.P. (2001) Institutional racism in British Psychiatry, *Psychiatric Bulletin* 25: 244-247

Scarman Report, 1981, *The Brixton disorder 10-12 April 1981*, London: Penguin Books

Sharpely, M.S. & Peters, E. (1999) Ethnicity, class and schizotypy. *Social Psychiatry and Psychiatric Epidemiology,* 34, 507-512.

Sharpley, M., Hutchinson, G., Murray, R.M. and McKenzie, k. (2001) Understanding the excess of psychosis among the African Caribbean population in England: review of current hypothesis', *British Journal of Psychiatry*, 178 (Supl. 40) pp. s60-s68)

Simon, R.J., Fleiss, J.L., Garland, R.J., Stiller, P.R. and Sharpe, L. (1973). 'Depression and schizophrenia in hospitalised Black and white mental patients,' *Archives of General Psychiatry,* 28, 509-12

Soloff, P.H. and Turner, S. M. (1981). 'Patterns of seclusion: a prosepective study', *Journal of Nervous and Mental Disease,* 169, 1 37-44.

Stephen, S. (1996) The Need for the re-education of the Black community', *Journal of Black Therapy,* 1, 2, 29-31.

Sugarman, P. A. & Craufurd, D. (1994) Schizophrenia in the Afro-Caribbean community. *British Journal of Psychiatry,* 164, 474-480.

University of Manchester, Department of Health, (1996) *Learning Materials on Mental Health, An Introduction,* Manchester: University of Manchester.

White, A. (2002) *Social Focus in Brief: Ethnicity*, London: Office for National Statistics

William- Morris, R. S. (1996) Racism and children's health: issues in development. *Ethnicity and Disease,* 6, 69-81.

The Blacks have become white!!!!

In the summer of 2011, a major controversy was caused when History Professor **David Starkey** appeared on BBC programme *Newsnight* to discuss the causes of that year's inner city riots. It was Starkey contention that the rules of civil society had broken down because of the negative influence of the children of Caribbean immigrants; that the traditionally law-abiding white working-class had been infected by the lawlessness of their Jamaican 'Yardie' neighbours. He was horrified that young whites were now dressing, talking and ultimately behaving like these glamorously anti-establishment migrants; in his own words, that the 'whites had become black'.

I would argue the opposite view to Starkey's. I would contend that many of the problems that plague Black men in Britain today, are because they have become *too white*. Or to be more precise, they have abandoned the values of those hard-working, law-abiding Caribbean immigrants of the Windrush generation, and taken on the values of the white working-class. Thus they no longer have that immigrant mentality of accepting whatever work you can get (no matter how menial), and scrimping and saving for a brighter future for their children. (That role is now left to the Eastern European migrants). This second and third generation of Caribbean immigrants, like the natives of this country, have a

sense of entitlement.   They feel that after their parents and grandparents worked so hard to rebuild this country, and paid their taxes for so many years, they now have an automatic right to a good education and a good home and a good job. And when the good things in life are not so easily forthcoming, they refuse to eat humble pie, and make do and mend as their grandparents may have done, and in some cases are willing to take what they want by force. (This difference between the immigrant mentality, and the mentality of the English natives which Black Britons have adopted, first became apparent to me when working in Wormwood Scrubs Prison as I discussed in chapter 2.) What unified those urban rioters in the summer of 2011, was not their race – it was their sense of entitlement coupled with a lack of opportunity. Like most young people they want designer label clothes and expensive trainers, high-tech smart phones and flat screen TVs, but with no job they are without the means to acquire them legally.

All of the problems that I have tackled in this book, from family breakdown, to educational underachievement, to mental illness are not problems of race, but problems of poverty. Why Black people seem to suffer them in larger numbers than the rest of society is because Black people are disproportionately concentrated in areas of poverty.

As we saw in Chapter 3, many of the gangs of London are concentrated in areas where there is a high Black population. But what connects these areas to districts in Glasgow where there are also a lot of gangs but no Black people, is the poverty and lack of opportunity. In essence gangs are not a 'Black thing', they are a 'ghetto thing'.

It is my contention that Black boys fare so badly in the school system not because they are Black but because they are poor. Yes Black boys are disproportionately excluded from school, but so are poor white boys. If it were just down to racist teachers or a racially biased curriculum then the children of Chinese and Indian immigrants would suffer similarly, but they don't. Data collected in the 90's showed that Indian students were most likely to achieve 5 or more passes at GCSE grade A – C; - that's more so even than white students.

Research shows that although ethnicity, socio-economic status and gender are all characteristics that affect educational experiences and results, the most influential factor is socio-economic status. At secondary school the differences between poorer and richer children is three times as great as the difference between children from different ethnic backgrounds who are equally disadvantaged. (Gilborn, 2008).

Only 21% of the poorest fifth (measured by parental socioeconomic position) manage to gain 5 good GCSE's, but for the richest fifth it is 75%.

The reason that no one makes a fuss about all the white working class boys being excluded from school is that most of the teachers who excluded them also happen to be white.

Yes Black men are overrepresented in the prison population, but so are poor white men. The reason that no one makes a fuss about all the white working class men in prison is that white men also dominate the police force and law courts that put them there. But when Black boys are disproportionately excluded from schools where most of the teachers are white, or are disproportionately subject to stop and search where most of the policemen are white, or disproportionately diagnosed as schizophrenic when most of the doctors and psychiatrists are white, then the issue of race is bound to raise its head.

We can expect that despite the similar crises facing Black people in America, the children of the super-rich Black elites will be insulated from such problems. We can reasonably expect that the daughters of Barack and Michelle Obama need not be overly concerned about teenage pregnancy and single parenthood. Or that the children of Will Smith and Jada Pinkett will not need to worry too much about getting excluded from school. Or the offspring of Jay

Z and Beyonce will be plagued by a life or gangs and jail. The fame, power and money of these African-American superstars does not stop them from being Black, but it does stop them from being poor, and so insulates their children from the challenges and pitfalls faced by so many others of their race. Not that you need a lot of money to do well in school, but you do need to have access to a good learning environment. A teenage girl doesn't need to be rich to avoid getting pregnant (family planning is free in this country) but if you live in a ghetto environment with its accompanying poverty of aspiration, then being a teenage single mother may be the height of your ambition. Poverty is a state of mind as well as the state of your finances.

So the overarching solution to all the problems detailed in this book, is to escape the ghettos on the mind as well as the sink estates. Easier said than done I know, but it important to acknowledge that poverty is a relative concept, not an absolute one, as anyone who has seen 'real poverty' in the developing world can attest to.

Printed in Great Britain
by Amazon